MANAGING TO RELATE

Interpersonal Skills at Work

STEPHEN C. SCHOONOVER, M.D.

Addison-Wesley Publishing Company Inc.
Reading, Massachusetts   Menlo Park, California   New York
Don Mills, Ontario   Wokingham, England   Amsterdam
Bonn   Sydney   Singapore   Tokyo   Madrid
San Juan

The publisher offers discounts on this book when ordered in quantity for special sales. For more information please contact:
Corporate & Professional Publishing Group
Addison-Wesley Publishing Company
Route 128
Reading, Massachusetts 01867

Library of Congress Cataloging-in-Publication Data
Schoonover, Stephen C., 1947–
  Managing to relate.

  Includes index.
  1. Psychology, Industrial. 2. Interpersonal relations. I. Title.
  HF5548.8.S353 1988   650.1′ 3   87-31417

Portions of Chapter 4 are adapted with permission from material copyrighted by Organizational Dynamics, Inc. © 1983

Copyright © 1988 by Addison-Wesley Publishing Co.

All rights reserved. No part of this publication may be reproduced, stored in a retrieval system, or transmitted, in any form or by any means, electronic, mechanical, photocopying, recording, or otherwise, without the prior written permission of the publisher. Printed in the United States of America. Published simultaneously in Canada.

Cover design by Jane Cook
Text design by Joyce C. Weston
Set in 11 point Sabon by Pine Tree Composition, Lewiston, ME

ISBN 0-201-15781-0

23456789-MU-93210

Second Printing, December 1990

Contents

Acknowledgments   v

Preface   vi

Introduction: Why Interpersonal Skills?   1

1. Harnessing the Power of Relationships   7

2. Interaction   23

3. Inquiry   48

4. Directive Influence   76

5. Strategic Influence   101

6. The 4-Is at Work   127

7. Personalizing the 4-Is   144

Epilogue: Fit To Lead   159

Appendix   165

Index   180

To Ellen, Danny and Sarah

Acknowledgments

I owe thanks to many people without whose support and wisdom this book would not have been possible. First of all, I am grateful to my wife, Ellen Bassuk, for her important suggestions about theoretical concepts and for her forbearance of the deadlines and other exigencies required for finishing the manuscript. In addition, I am especially thankful for the administrative, emotional, and practical help given by Mary Nell Schoonover.

Others were vital for sharpening concepts too. Murray Dalziel, Helen Vandkjaer, and Patricia Rieker provided important feedback about the 4-I model during early stages of its development. Mary Lou Balbake offered early test sites during instrument testing. Naomi Steinberg and John Pendergrass gave ongoing support during several phases of model refinement and data collection. In addition, they generated critical feedback from course participants at various test sites and offered many clarifying comments of their own.

Finally, I owe deep thanks to Russell Schutt for data analysis and the wisdom he shared to refine the 4-I instrument, as well as the interpretation of study results at each stage of concept development.

Preface

Interpersonal skills are the basis for all management practices. They represent the foundation of productive work and employee satisfaction. This book presents a model for understanding and mastering interpersonal skills—the 4-I Model of Interpersonal Skills. The model, grounded in behavioral science research from a number of settings with a wide range of individuals doing different types of work, provides an easy-to-understand framework that can be applied readily to practical job situations.

The model defines four types of interpersonal skills—interaction, inquiry, directive influence, and strategic influence—to create a framework for confronting interpersonal barriers in the workplace. It provides a method for diagnosing personal vulnerabilities and developing strategies for confronting specific situations. Most important, the model can help leaders with day-to-day concerns and long-term skill development.

The book is organized by several principles:

1. It has four tracks along which vital principles are presented:
   - A fast track provides the busy manager with a

quick overview through bulleted summaries and the summary figures at the end of each chapter;
- A more detailed track gives a comprehensive picture of interpersonal skills and self-improvement strategies through the text and the cases;
- A segmented track helps a person improve one skill area or one type of management situation by reviewing one of the four skill clusters of the 4-I model in detail;
- A comprehensive developmental track includes reviewing the model, learning about applications, and modifying key concepts according to the leader's personality and experience.
2. Each skill cluster is presented in a separate chapter, and each skill is explained in its own segment.
3. The body of the text is divided into five main parts—a first chapter that provides an overview of the interpersonal skills model; four chapters that present the 4-I model; a chapter on applications to refine skills; a chapter on developing skills through personal change; and a final chapter that explores how refining interpersonal skills can bring about greater business success.
4. At the end of the book, an appendix documents the research that helped develop and validate the model and its key principles.

In any management situation, leaders can improve their level of functioning by asking basic questions about their business environment:

- Do people *trust* each other enough to share openly and take emotional and creative chances?

viii • PREFACE

- Do I know the *problems to be solved* and the *possibilities to pursue* in my job area?
- Do I share a clear, *specific set of directions* for productive work with coworkers?
- Can I *implement plans* effectively through the people I lead?

This book offers managers a way to answer these questions and a step-by-step method for developing the interpersonal strategies to master these four dimensions—trust, a focus for action, directions, and actions for implementing new ideas.

Managing to Relate is meant to be read, used, and re-used. It is designed as a practical companion that is both a quick and easy reference and a comprehensive, data-based framework for improving management and leadership effectiveness.

Introduction: Why Interpersonal Skills?

Business as Un-usual

During the 1980s, the United States has gone from being a major creditor nation to being a major debtor nation, owing hundreds of billions of dollars to the rest of the world. Although the hemorrhage of economic security and prosperity stems mostly from a loss in the U.S. competitive position in manufacturing, it now appears vulnerable in key service sectors too. Experts have noted many contributions to the United States' present problems, such as a lower per capita investment in research and development than its major competitors, a low savings rate and wasteful consumption in the general population, deficit spending by the government, and poor quality and productivity in its workforce. One of the most alarming factors in the equation of the present competitive dilemma is untapped, ineffective, inefficient leadership. This book focuses on developing the foundation for excellent leadership—interpersonal skills.

The present business climate has demanded a remarkable transformation—flatter organizations, more projects and processes requiring collaboration between coworkers, more frequent and dramatic change initiatives, quicker shifts in strategic direction, and more rapid prod-

2 • MANAGING TO RELATE

uct and process development. In addition, significant cutbacks in staffing and decreased layers of management make personal competence for adapting to ever-changing business, interpersonal, and group demands the rule, not the exception.

Today's corporations abound with new kinds of opportunities, but must also confront the problems that result from building systems open to information and ideas. Quality circles, collaborative work practices, even fewer walls and doors in office settings are intended to increase personal contact. Electronic mail, voice message transmission, and computerized document handling, storage, and manipulation all speed information flow. But these changes also can impede interpersonal communication. For example, the new computerized methods of information exchange may serve as a barrier to effective enterprise—a kind of "digital reality" in which data forms and electronic and printed messages overload the system. Softer, face-to-face human contact may be explicitly or implicitly ignored. In many settings, passing attention is paid to the interpersonal dimensions of the workplace with homilies about the importance of listening or participative management. These do not provide lasting behavior change. Instead, concepts are soon forgotten, and management goes back to "real" work. Why is this? Mostly because the neglect of human resources, in general, and interpersonal skills, in particular, does not have an immediate impact on the bottom line.

Research shows that deficits in personal and group skills do have profound effects but that these effects take five to ten years to surface. At first, problems with morale and job satisfaction appear. Then, operational difficulties emerge. Finally, the bottom line suffers as interpersonal problems start to have widespread impact. Because these weaknesses take years to develop, negligent organizations may not be able to regroup for skill development fast enough to remain competitive once their vulnerability is discovered.

For example, an international manufacturing power decided to cut costs to remain competitive in a worldwide marketplace. It decreased layers of management; it offered early retirement for some employees and severance pay for others; it consolidated operations into fewer divisions; it even sold some of its less profitable businesses. Although the focus was exclusively on the bottom line, employees became afraid, demoralized, and even less productive. The company continued to have problems meeting the costs of competitors' products and redoubled its efforts at cost cutting. With even more work and less attention to personal concerns and relationships, individual productivity and quality suffered. Finally, the slide in market share forced the corporation to overhaul its top management.

In contrast, a similar corporation took many of the same initiatives, but during the transition it devoted additional resources to communication between management levels, to retraining and skill development, and most important to helping people rethink, discuss, and develop new ways of directing their own careers. This corporationwide dialogue not only validated the employees' right to express concerns but also offered methods for reframing their relationship with the corporation. The loss of some "old" values, such as lifetime employment, was significant. However, a new—perhaps less paternalistic—

relationship was formed between employees and the company.

Tomorrow's Leaders

As a response to the many changes in business, leadership has also become a rallying cry for corporations—and rightfully so. New, flexible organizational structures, open communications, responsibility without authority, and change put personal leadership center stage. No longer can businesses rely on traditional management structures for smooth operations. Even the implicit promise that computers would be companions in management has proven elusive at best. But what kind of leadership do we need?

Management and academics alike have called for leaders who can transform, who can "do the right things, not just do things right," who can think strategically, who can use "visioning" to see future possibilities. Although these characteristics are most commonly attributed to natural leaders in top management positions, the new workplace requires leaders at every organizational level.

So-called visionary leaders sometimes focus on results —and occasionally their own self-aggrandizement—to the exclusion of reiationship building. All too often, they make mandates for change that focus on large-scale interventions—ignoring both the needs of individuals and the collective power of people to invigorate businesses. As a young manàger in a computer firm noted, "Upper management calls its competitive strategies 'vision,' but I call them problems that I have to solve one at a time. Mostly, creativity and effective outcomes happen at a personal level—through people who are committed to excellence because I have a relationship with them."

Introduction: Why Interpersonal Skills? • 5

The current leaders who must produce day-to-day results face unique challenges. They must embrace innovative changes and reaffirm the importance of people at the same time. But how? In a constantly changing, collaborative work setting, leaders must not only create visions but also mobilize people to implement those visions. In most cases, the primary barrier to change is not the lack of vision, but the lack of interpersonal skills. As one vice-president of a major manufacturing corporation recently told me, "We've got a vision of the future; we just don't have enough leaders with the people skills to get us there."

By some expert accounts, two-thirds of the failures that occur in organizational settings stem not from technical or structural deficits but from failures in relationships. For example, a recent study we did on project leaders for an international manufacturing firm showed that personal attributes—such as team-building skills, techniques for persuasion and ownership-building, and concern for the timing and impact of interventions—were much more responsible for the success of projects than technical or managerial skills.

Interpersonal skills, always a cohesive force in businesses, have now become a vital competitive necessity. This book presents a simple model for learning, using, and improving interpersonal skills at work. Based on a well-researched, easy-to-use method, called the *4-I Model of Interpersonal Skills,* the book highlights a number of basic concepts about people and relationships.

The interpersonal skills model, comprised of four basic skill groups, specifies how to *mix, sequence,* and *refine* interpersonal behavior to fit individual relationships and situations. Because it offers both a comprehensive framework and an easily remembered picture of interpersonal skills, the 4-I model can serve many purposes for the busy leader. It can be used as a situational leadership guide, a self-improvement tool, a coaching and counseling aid, even a career development tool. No matter what help the model provides for you personally, it can significantly improve your ability to understand, assess, and change your own and others' interpersonal behavior.

1

Harnessing the Power of Relationships

Relating Is Mostly Work; Work Is Mostly Relating

Ernest was considered a quality performer at ATCO. He was an upright, toe-the-mark, three-piece-suited citizen who took managing seriously. His division was making record profits from drug sales, but some of his reps were starting to slip.

Sally, a sales rep coming for a performance review, wasn't meeting quota in her drug sales. With two hospitals in her area sold to national chains and all of her other accounts on crusades of cost-cutting, she was failing more often even though she was trying harder. Sally was worried and having a lot of trouble keeping up in all areas of her life—marriage, mothering, self-image, and selling.

Ernest had learned the importance of starting meetings with a welcoming touch—particularly when you have to deliver "bad" news. So he met Sally at his door. "Good morning, Sally. How are you today?"

Sally straightened visibly, trying to look as upbeat as possible. She replied, "Oh, fine. And you?"

"I'm pretty good," Ernest responded. "Come on in and let's get down to business! Today, I'd like to go over your

8 • MANAGING TO RELATE

quota and the accounts in your area, so we can make a realistic action plan that gets those sales up. OK?"

"Well, OK," Sally replied slowly. Her head bent a little lower. She could see Ernest was going by the books, and it didn't provide a pretty picture. She thought to herself, "Why can't he see how many obstacles I've had to overcome and how hard I'm trying?"

Ernest went on. "You were meeting quota up until last year. Now, let's talk about some ways to get back on track."

Sally felt hurt, even a little angry. Her sales were actually higher than a year ago. But every year a persons' sales increase, their quota jumps no matter what's happening in the real world. You could win—and get a bonus—only if you increased sales every single year!

Ernest continued. "Sally, Sally . . . You seem distracted. Now, what do you think you can do to help us both succeed?"

Ernest looked earnest; Sally looked beaten.

Ernest was proud of himself. He'd greeted Sally warmly. At least, he thought so. He got to the point without wasting time. He focused on the problem, not Sally's personality. He kept his own frustrations out of the meeting.

Sally took Ernest's attempt at efficient management badly. She was already on the defensive because he was so damned efficient—so matter-of-fact, so unemotional. Her whole life was a mess, her career was crumbling, and she couldn't control it, and Ernest was acting like a robot. Ernest had followed all the rules for good performance feedback; he punched the right buttons. But he did a lousy job without even noticing because he failed to connect with Sally in a way that resonated with her own personal concerns.

The People Connection

Do you really make personal contact with people in your day-to-day activities? Without hesitation, the answer is no for most of us. It certainly was for Ernest.

You have probably noticed that some individuals establish connections with other people naturally. They are warmer and more gracious, more people-oriented than others. These natural "helpers" establish rapport without effort. Studies show that in every environment—office, neighborhood, family—one or more individuals stand out because they like talking and listening, and they instinctively understand and sympathize.

You have probably also observed other individuals who are natural at getting things done. They use relationships for a functional purpose, to reach goals and achieve results. In contrast to "helpers," born "implementors" have the ability to inspire and motivate others toward productive goals. They often become the high achievers, the entrepreneurs, or charismatic leaders that give businesses their competitive edge.

But most individuals are neither born helpers nor born implementors. For them, superior people skills are not a natural gift. Instead, they struggle to find common ground with the people they work with and labor to find an effective means of influence. Fortunately, however, interpersonal skills can be learned and developed. By changing even the smallest of behaviors, you can significantly alter the outcomes of your interactions with other people.

What Miscommunicates?

Although interpersonal skills can be learned, they cannot be learned quickly or easily. Mechanical skills, such as learning to use a computer, are relatively straightforward. The computer does not change from day to day, and the process of operating it remains constant. People skills, in contrast, take place in a continually changing environment between people who are growing and developing. In addition, the jargon, clothes, titles, and management techniques people use to protect themselves often blind us to their real motivations and feelings, making it difficult for us to decide what behavior would be appropriate and effective.

Another complexity of interpersonal skills is that verbal communication is only a fraction of the interchange that takes place between two people. For example, a one-year study of verbal communication among couples happily married for more than fifteen years found that they did not talk much—in fact, an average of only twenty-seven and a half minutes per week! However, they connected frequently and accurately through ongoing patterns of communication—specific sequences of action and inaction. For these marriages, effective communication was coded into both actions and words. In discussing his home life, one manager stated, "I can tell my wife's mood within ten seconds of walking in the door. Even before I say hello. Her walk, her movement, the way she does the dishes or cleans up, even the way she chews food. She has a nervous chew, an angry chew, a contented chew. One chew is worth a thousand words!"

We communicate on many different levels—speech tempo, volume, intonation, facial expressions, limb

Harnessing the Power of Relationships • 11

movements, posture, and interpersonal distance all influence and may even decide the meaning of a communication. This multichanneled nature of communications can increase clarity or cause confusion. Redundancy—or the presentation of a message in many forms at the same time—can either ensure that communication occurs more effectively or impart contradictory messages. For example, when someone offers a welcome with words, a smile, a comfortable setting, and appropriate caretaking, each form of communication builds on the others. In contrast, Sally's manager Ernest used the right words and followed form but failed to ensure a comfortable environment for talking and failed to take the time to adopt Sally's perspective. He gave the impression—intended or not—of being more interested in following the proper management protocol than in helping Sally.

Even when people make every effort to relate effectively, confounding factors always operate to potentially distort what people say or hear. Personalities can cause confusions. In the instance of Sally, her manager Ernest's by-the-books approach failed to establish trust and rapport prior to proceeding to a dialogue about performance feedback.

The communication cross-currents caused by setting, situation, and cultural cues also have profound effects. For example, an American anthropologist who was eating dinner with Iranian friends was asked if she wanted a second helping. Still hungry, but knowing that polite Iranians go through a ritual of multiple refusals before accepting more food, she declined. The Iranians, sensitive to the fact that Americans respond more directly to offers of food and not wanting to offend their guest, did not offer again. The American, not wanting to be impolite, made no further requests. The result—a hungry but polite anthropologist. The sensitive anthropologist and her equally sensitive hosts misunderstood one another because they were filtering communications through different cultural premises.

In an organizational setting, relationships simultaneously serve many purposes besides manifest business agendas. Friendships are formed. Feelings of "family" are developed. Mentors are found. In the midst of these relationships, people inevitably develop, maintain, or suppress their self-esteem. Sometimes personal problems and esteem-lowering interactions fill the role of a bad attachment or what might be called a "chronic self-defeating transaction or habit." In this case, a cycle is formed: By paying attention to some cues and ignoring others, a person can continually reinforce his or her misperceptions. This in turn fuels poor relating habits that inevitably result in negative responses from others that confirm the person's initial poor self-image.

For example, some people repeatedly become "victims" by complying with unfair or sadistic behavior. Some become "janitors" for the problems of others because they instinctively clean other people's messes. Some become leaders because they sense and seek opportunities for exercising power. Along with the tendency for people to live out their own stories in relationships, each interpersonal exchange is affected by group norms, values, and issues. Some experts, for instance, think that the recent breakdown in ethics in business stems not from individual pettiness but from a wide discrepancy in the level of rewards that people receive for their work. Living in a world of haves and have-nots seems to promote strong self-interest at the expense of group or team goals. At an interpersonal level, this means less empathy, less interest in the perspective of others, and much more concern about influence and manipulation.

Poor communication and faulty interpersonal skills are pervasive social problems. Unethical activities, failed plans, demoralized organizations, even social upheavals and war result from failed relationships. People wittingly and unwittingly abuse and confuse others. Even a highly motivated leader has a daunting job in trying to assess and respond to the myriad, unfolding variables that comprise a relationship.

What are Interpersonal Skills?

Words and movements are the primary communication vehicles in interpersonal relations. But interpersonal skills are more than just communication. At the most basic level, they are special kinds of effective behaviors—ways that people influence and respond sensitively to one another. These skills are not just simple actions and responses, but a complex pattern of behaviors that fit each interaction between individuals and each context. The process of relating well rests on an array of attitudes, knowledge, and actions—both verbal and nonverbal—each tailored to the task, the setting, the personality, mood, and behaviors of those being influenced. One experienced manager captured the complexity of interpersonal skills: "You've got to be involved with other people and be aware of yourself and your setting all at the same time. You've got to talk and listen, be receptive and assert your own point of view. And you've got to make your responses fit what's going on at the moment. Obviously, I fail a lot."

But on a practical level what are interpersonal skills?

14 • MANAGING TO RELATE

Interpersonal skills are best represented as a quadrant framework, using the two basic qualities of all interpersonal skills as the axes. (See Figure 1–1.)

The vertical axis in the figure defines what is being discussed. When individuals focus on people-oriented subjects, such as subjective feelings, perspectives, and concerns, they are using skills that are located at one end of the axis. When focusing on task or concept-oriented concerns, such as work problems, goals, or activities, the skills used are located at the other end.

The horizontal axis defines how the speaker is conducting dialogue. When a person primarily takes an ac-

Figure 1–1: What to Say and How to Say It

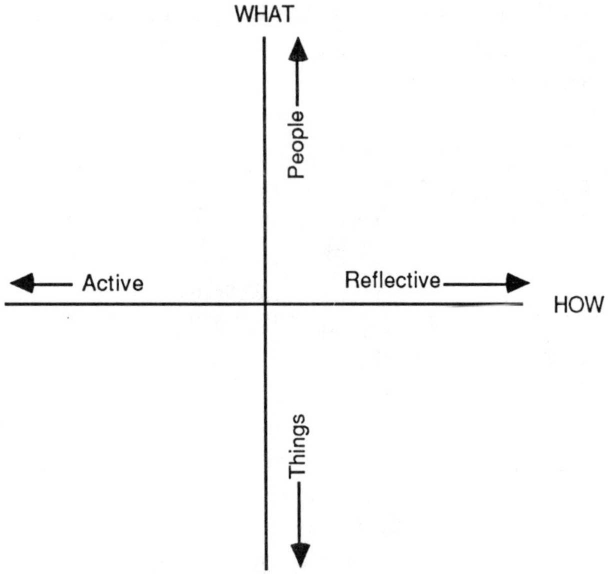

tive stance—one in which he or she acts frequently or assertively—the skills used lie at one end of the axis. A reflective stance lies at the other. These two axes—*what* (from an orientation toward people and feelings to an orientation toward tasks and concepts) and *how* (from an active to a reflective stance)—combine to generate four quadrants, each defining a major skill area or cluster: interaction, inquiry, directive and strategic influence. (See Figure 1–2.) This surface or map is the framework for the 4-I model of interpersonal skills.

The first *I* or skill cluster, *interaction,* is defined by those interpersonal behaviors that are most people-

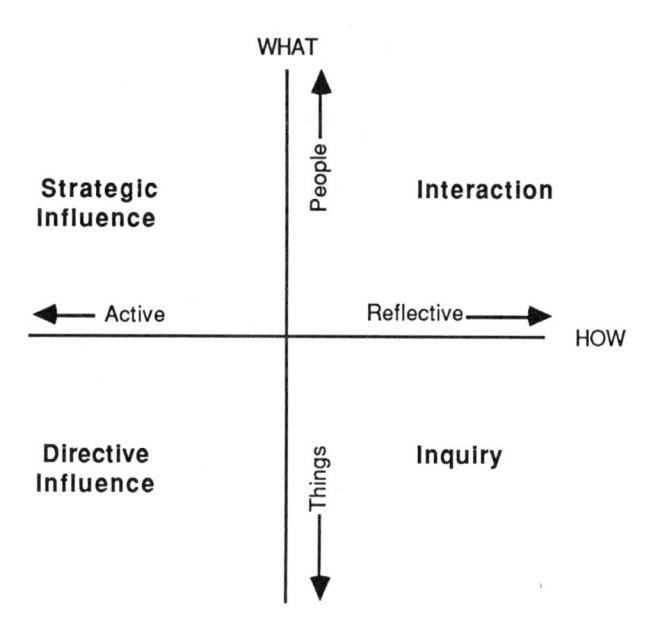

Figure 1–2: The 4-I Model of Interpersonal Skills

	WHAT (People)	
Strategic Influence		**Interaction**
← Active		Reflective → HOW
Directive Influence		**Inquiry**
	Things ↓	

oriented and most reflective. These interpersonal skills are helpful in therapeutic, counseling, and coaching situations. The second *I, inquiry,* is defined by those behaviors that are most reflective and fact or task-oriented. These skills are useful in circumstances requiring information-gathering or focusing on problems or opportunities. The third *I, directive influence,* is defined by those behaviors that are most active and task or fact-oriented. These skills are important in giving directions, confronting problems, and making plans. The fourth *I, strategic influence,* is comprised of the most active and people-oriented set of skills. These are required for motivating others and implementing activities. Together, these four skills clusters and the map they form can be used to assess whether or not situational demands are being addressed most effectively.

All interpersonal skills have three behavioral dimensions—the *mix* or combination of behaviors demonstrated, the *sequencing* or order of behaviors, and the *personal refinements* or subtleties in each interchange that put a personal stamp on the discussion. All three dimensions or communication channels work in concert for the most effective results.

Learning the general boundaries or map of behaviors needed for each situational context is a prerequisite for effective interpersonal skills. For example, an individual building trust with another person should take a calm, attentive, reflective stance and avoid controlling, directive, manipulative behaviors. In contrast, the map for situations that require selling ideas is comprised of more persuasion, feedback, and giving advice; relationship-building behaviors are limited to the extent necessary for getting approval for the agenda at hand.

The second behavioral dimension of interpersonal skills is sequencing or order. Every goal-directed dialogue is meant to change the listener in some important way. To change requires "movement" or direction. In relationships this is accomplished through a set of steps or *sequences* of behaviors. For example, part of every problem-solving process entails generating options. This often proceeds in steps from defining the problem to offering relatively unstructured opinions to clarifying concepts and possibilities to specifying corrective actions. The process moves from unformed ideas to defined activities and commitments.

For all business agendas there is a basic direction that underlies all relationships. The four stages of every process include: establishing trust; specifying a focus for action; developing directions; and implementing actions. Each good relating process is a reiteration of this basic pattern. In other words, each relationship naturally moves through a set of challenges or issues from trust to a focus to directions to actions.

This pattern follows the framework for the 4-I model. Trust is primarily developed through interaction skills; a common focus through inquiry skills; agreement about directions through directive influence; and generation of actions in others through strategic influence. (See Figures 1–3 and 1–4.)

For example, to complete sales cycles, effective leaders move prospects through all four issues but in a limited, focused manner. They develop trust in proportion to the amount of security the prospect needs to place an order. They gather enough information to define customer needs. They develop a direction, a plan, a strategy toward a potential commitment by establishing "fit" be-

18 • MANAGING TO RELATE

Figure 1-3: Model of the 4-I Interpersonal Skills: The Four Relating Issues

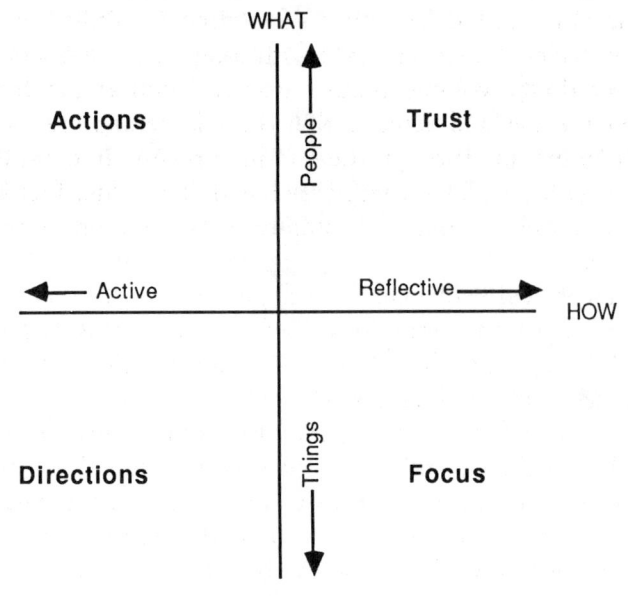

Figure 1-4: The Four Relating Issues

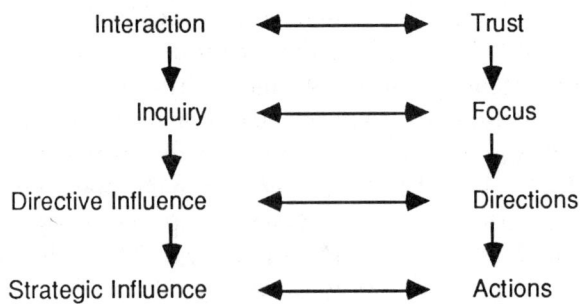

tween customer needs and product benefits. Finally, they ask for the order after influencing the customer to buy through carefully tailored persuasion and feedback. The general process or sequence of relating is fulfilled in all sales cycles. However, sales with long-term contracts or larger dollar volume require deeper commitment from the customer and demand that the salesperson use more care in moving through the relating process. In contrast, sales with a smaller volume or less dollar value, focused efforts, yielding quicker commitments are more appropriate.

In a typical management cycle, leaders must also move through the four relating issues. (See Figure 1–5, page 21.) Mobilizing the network for information and resources, and building a work team requires trust. Defining a work focus requires inquiry. Setting and meeting goals, timelines, and milestones require directive influence. Motivating coworkers to implement key activities requires strategic influence. Again, the basic pattern of relating is followed in sequence, but at a deeper level with more individuals over a longer period of time.

Providing mentorship requires a different view of the same basic process. Because individual development occurs over a period of many months, even years, a mentor must fulfill each relating issue at a very deep, detailed, personal level to produce significant change. In addition to moving slowly through the hierarchy of issues, a leader must reintegrate the steps in relating many times as crises and new opportunities necessitate personal reappraisal.

In the real world, the sequence, the emphasis on each step, and even the nature of each step may vary. However, in all instances, a relating process that evolves over time must occur. And it generally corresponds to the steps or process required to resolve one or more of the four relating issues.

The third behavioral dimension entails personal refinements. Perhaps most relationship problems stem from a deficit of skill performance—an inability to demonstrate competent behaviors in a refined way. At a practical level, this occurs when a leader is not specific, subtle, or consistent in using an interpersonal skill. For example, one of the most important behaviors for all leaders is acceptance of their employees. This demands an abiding tolerance of others' opinions and idiosyncracies over long periods of time to engender credibility. Small actions done repeatedly, such as saying hello, addressing people by their first name, asking what people think and feel about their work, make a very big difference. But if a leader performs these actions without subtlety or in a mechanical, perfunctory way, they will have limited impact.

Although people frequently fail to learn interpersonal skills, more often they fail to apply skills consistently. Because a relationship is not a single event but instead a series of reciprocal feedback processes that occur over time, each moment theoretically requires a new skill mix to fit changing demands. This ideal is unreachable, but people can significantly improve how they communicate by effecting small changes in behavior. For example, Ernest could have solidified a significant alliance with Sally if he had simply taken the time to ask about her thoughts and feelings before getting down to business. Two or three open-ended questions and five minutes of listening would have changed the tone of the meeting and improved Sally's morale. Sally also failed to respond appropriately. She could have stopped Ernest from alienating her by asking him to listen to her perspective before discussing solutions to problems. Subordinates, like Sally, sometimes adopt a passive stance, expecting their managers to guide relationships in consistently productive directions. The 4-I model provides a means for discovering and confronting vulnerabilities, such as those of Ernest and Sally.

All those who work in a corporate context are assigned

Figure 1-5: The Management Cycle

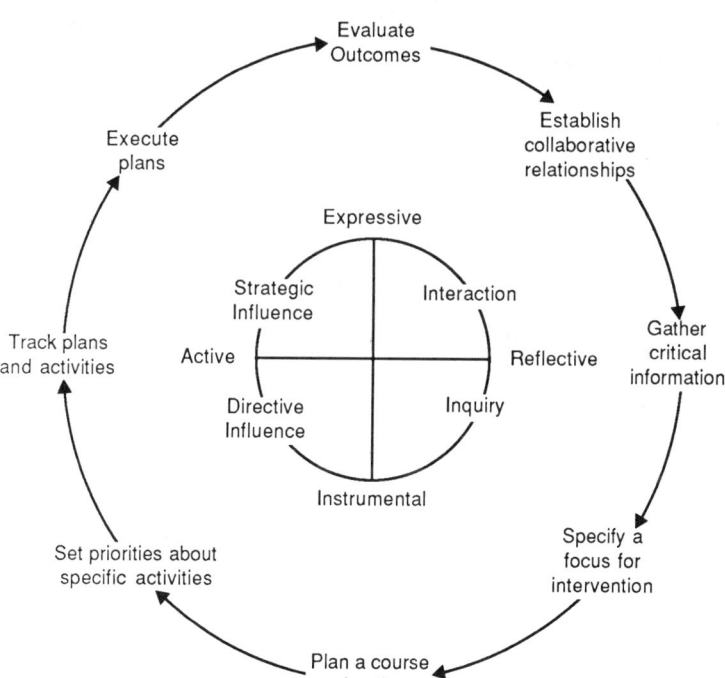

specific job tasks and roles. But they get the job done by means of their words, gestures, movements, and interactions with others. The 4-I model helps leaders know when to apply and when to resist or modify the application of behaviors. In practical terms, the model is a framework to help improve the mixing, sequencing, and refinement of interpersonal behaviors required for various demands of the job. The 4-Is make new attitudes and behaviors easy to learn. They provide a motivating framework for remembering and applying skills—a bridge for sharing values, beliefs, themes, and goals. And they help leaders address the basic issues that underlie all relationships. In the following chapters, we explore each of the four skill clusters in depth and see how they can be applied in all business settings.

2

Interaction

Interaction is the set of interpersonal skills that produces trust between people. These behaviors are reflective and focus on individuals—their thoughts, sensitivities, subjective perspectives, and feelings. Interaction is most important for building and repairing relationships, forming and maintaining teams, and intervening with individuals in ways such as coaching, counseling, and feedback sessions.

"I'm Not Your Mom!"

Milt was the consummate manager—charismatic, energetic, committed, action-oriented, attentive to the details and milestones that make things happen. As a result, he had led several project teams that designed and introduced new products. He often referred to himself as being "authoritative without being authoritarian."

About a year ago, Milt was asked to head a team to design and implement automated processes in a factory. Leslie, a bright, young engineer, lobbied to work on the project—on Milt's team.

The first day was like launching a ship. Milt had a real sense of fanfare. He gave an inspirational speech about how technological "leaps" were the only way to stay ahead of the competition. The sense of excitement and expectation was palpable. Directions were charted, tasks defined, and roles assigned. The team was formed and plans were made without a hitch.

As the project proceeded, problems occurred as they inevitably do. Several team members complained that they were feeling uneasy, uncertain about their roles and how they were doing. Leslie, in particular, became increasingly disgruntled. In one encounter, she approached Milt cautiously and said, "I know the results you want, but I feel you're really not with us."

Milt looked bewildered and replied, "I'm not sure what you mean."

Leslie was visibly put off. She had taken a big risk in confronting someone who was the head of her team and very much her senior in the organization. She glanced from side to side as she pondered her next move. Then she replied, "Uh . . . I don't think you really have a sense of the problems we're having. You're so quick that you're in and out before you have a chance to hear us out on things."

Milt had heard this kind of complaint before. So he quickly passed it off saying, "I'm here to get results, not to be a mom or a therapist. People naturally want to schmooze and waste time. Sometimes I seem a little coldhearted, but I think it produces the best results."

When Milt responded in such a cursory, matter-of-fact manner and used the third person to refer to her, Leslie became angry. She pursed her lips. Milt effectively silenced her, but at a tremendous cost. Milt lost an vital alliance with his engineer.

Milt was a real dynamo, a pacesetter. But he always was a little distant from people. When asked later how she felt about Milt, Leslie said, "I feel like he's running for office. I just stick to business and go through the motions with him because he is pretty impervious to my worries." Milt was told, (off the record) that he had all the tools to succeed—except one. People wanted to work with him, but only once, because they felt used and didn't feel respected. His team generally felt alienated. Leslie felt that Milt "wanted a promotion, not a relationship."

In many ways, Milt is typical of busy managers—lots of pressure, little time for decisions, a bias toward action, and no one to provide feedback about how to relate more effectively. In this context, the issue of trust and closeness between coworkers is particularly nettlesome. What information and feelings are appropriate to share? How should people resolve the conflict between the demands of friendship and the exercise of authority? How can a leader be involved personally and objectively at the same time? Most often, organizations solve the dilemma through a kind of double standard. Participatory work practices, quality of work life initiatives, and collaboration are manifestly espoused. But in practice, leaders usually succumb to focusing on tasks and deadlines, not people or the group processes that achieve outcomes.

Most often, this tendency stems from the pressure of organizational demands and from a lack of competence and comfort with the skills required for *interaction*. Even though he sincerely tried, Milt failed in each of the four major interaction skills. He did not demonstrate

- *Attention* because he did not sense, assess, and respond to the cues Leslie gave during their discussions;

- *Empathy* because he was unable to put himself into Leslie's perspective;
- *Respect* because he was unable to provide a nonjudgmental holding environment in which Leslie could feel her concerns were legitimate;
- *Rapport* because he failed to develop and maintain a solid emotional connection with Leslie during their talks.

In a way, Leslie also failed because she allowed the flawed interaction to proceed.

The collusion between two people in not establishing trust is, in fact, very frequent. This happens partly because individuals have less control in relationships than they imagine. In interaction, the leader's primary role is that of a participant or facilitator rather than complete master of each agenda. A communicator does not just speak to a listener. In the process of interaction, each statement evokes a response, which in turn influences the form and content of the communicator's next response. Therefore, in interaction, more than any of the other skill groups, individuals need to continually refine their behavior, responding to the moment-to-moment needs for developing and maintaining trust with the other person. For example, the most empathic individuals can sense when the feeling state of the listener changes, even slightly, by tuning into subtle responses, such as hesitations in speech and changes in facial expression, muscle tension, or body position. More important, they then know how to adjust their own verbal and body language to reestablish contact. For many people these adjustments are automatic. But if you have less instinct for empathy, paying attention to the small cues that reveal how another person is responding to you can help guide you in selecting your subsequent responses.

All communication between people has this back and forth or reciprocal quality. It is the essence of the human bond or attachment. It can be either "symmetrical" or "complementary." Symmetrical relationships occur when participants share personal qualities or goals. In these instances, people tend to evoke equal or similar responses from one another. In practice, leaders maintain the continuity of the bond through interaction skills such as sharing feelings and ideas. The advantage of symmetrical communications is that they are agreeable. They tend to foster a friendly, easy-going atmosphere. However, they can also present devastating problems. Sometimes, when total agreement is not reached, relationships do not have the flexibility to adapt. Other times, the use of common terms (such as acronyms or buzz words), the suppression of conflict, or the sharing of maladaptive behavior produces symptoms such as "groupthink" or shared distortions. In these instances, effective leaders must step outside the relationship to find more productive ways of interacting.

Complementary relationships occur in the context of large differences of communication style or personality. Participants in this type of interchange tend to adopt polarized roles. Sometimes this is appropriate for efficiency and effectiveness. For example, in the best teams, members play various complementary roles. The entrepreneurs or inventors on a team who generate ideas and their business applications. They often benefit from being reined in by integrators and managers who insist that they consider much more organized and practical perspectives for easy implementation. In contrast, the extreme forms of complementary relationships are rigid and oppositional—representing struggles in which each person is more interested in holding a position than accomplishing effective communication.

To determine your own facility in forming a trusting bond, use the following checklist to rate your strengths and vulnerabilities. Do you

- Suspend judgment about your own opinions during conversation with others?
- Invest full attention to others?
- Act respectfully about others' ideas and opinions?
- Express ongoing interest and warmth toward others by paying attention to their feelings and ideas?
- Tune into what people think and feel but don't say out loud, such as negative or vulnerable thoughts?
- Adopt other people's perspective during conversation?
- Consistently focus on others' feelings and perceptions?
- Remain calm, relaxed, and attentive during conversation?
- Respond to and validate others' opinions and feelings?
- Maintain a positive attitude about others even when there is conflict or disagreement?

A significant deficit in any of these skills or moderate deficits in several will limit a leader's ability to establish, maintain, or reestablish trust in business relationships.

"Attending to Business": Attention

Attention—or the ability to sense, interpret, and respond to the many cues in the environment—is the natural companion to all other interaction skills. It is the skill that focuses on the assessment and interpretation of complex messages exchanged through words, body language, voice tone, and the coordination and discoordination between people who are relating. Perhaps the most basic of interpersonal skills, it is the bridge between raw communication and a leader's acute awareness of the factors that make relationships run effectively. As such, it is a facilitative skill—necessary but not used in a vacuum; it works in tandem with other interaction skills.

In many ways, attentiveness has a bad name in business circles. Seen as too mushy, too subjective, too time consuming, too distracting from important concerns, too unprofitable and downright "unbusinesslike," an attentive or receptive stance is in fact one of the critical keys to successful leadership. Attention has two major dimensions—one receptive; the other responsive. First of all, it relies on what some experts call *cue sensitivity* or a person's ability to detect important overt and covert communication in people. Attention helps to detect feelings, motives, ideas, possibilities and problems before they become manifest. As the middle manager of a banking firm pointed out, "My most important role is to regulate activities without being too controlling. Invariably, I do this by focusing on what people are feeling and doing and why. This way I pick up on potential creative opportunities before they're lost and potential problems before they're emergencies."

Besides developing a receptive attitude, the excellent leader also works at responding to others' feelings, opinions, and actions. This responsive part of attention is a two-way process supported by complex verbal and nonverbal behaviors. In practice, it is easy to get stuck in a limited view of interactions. One man described how he was derailed from paying attention by an annoying mannerism that his boss brought to each personal interaction:

> Every time we'd have a serious conversation, he'd pick at his finger nails. After awhile, I couldn't think of anything except breaking his hands. I couldn't keep focused on what we were talking about and I couldn't think of any way to confront or bypass his bad habit. Maybe it was his way of telling me something, but I just couldn't get past it.

Paying attention is not a passive pursuit but instead a series of detailed responses that keep communication channels open. In behavioral terms, excellent leaders monitor both nonverbal and verbal cues of their coworkers, and then respond by testing their understanding and reinforcing further dialogue. Much of this is accomplished with nonverbal cues. For example, good eye contact is one of the most important ways leaders can demonstrate attention and interest. Natural, direct eye-to-eye contact, particularly during emotional or sensitive topics, works best. This is, of course, a general guideline. Attentiveness can be taken too far also. One employee started calling his boss "Fish Eye" when he adopted a riveting stare after taking a listening course that encouraged direct eye contact.

Body and facial postures also can convey interest or disinterest. Think of the times that someone frowned or turned away from you while you were talking. What was the effect? On the other hand, a pleasant facial expression and a lean in the direction of the speaker often enhance a feeling of connection. In fact, many body signals impart a sense of interest. Among the most effective are

- Facing someone directly;
- Leaning toward them;
- Maintaining a relaxed body;
- Keeping the body (particularly the hands) still;
- Adopting a "warm" facial expression;
- Maintaining a comfortable physical distance.

Receptive and reinforcing body movements can encourage conversation and put coworkers at ease. How do you feel when someone interrupts a conversation with a halting gesture or when someone fidgets while you're talking? These are not invitations to openness. In contrast, many body and facial movements encourage continued and more open communication. Among the most effective are

- A change in facial expression or nodding of the head immediately following important comments;
- Comfortable, relaxed gestures that either reach toward coworkers or openly invite an approach from them (such as being "welcomed with open arms");
- Frequent sharing or "mirroring" of body positions or movements.

Milt could have been a more effective project leader if he had been more attentive to Leslie's concerns when they first talked. He missed multiple cues that could have warned him that Leslie did not trust him. From the start of their interaction, Leslie appeared cautious. Milt might have picked up on this, saying something, such as, "Leslie, are you a little worried? Why don't we talk about what's on your mind?" Later, when Leslie was visibly put off, Milt could have interjected, "I don't seem to be getting your point. Tell me some more about what you're thinking." And when Leslie was "glancing from side to side," Milt could have responded by asking a question or reflecting on Leslie's continued uneasiness with their interaction. In several instances, Milt had opportunities to build his personal credibility rather than continue to alienate Leslie.

Responsive behaviors are like a dance, and Milt was definitely out of step. The general maneuvers that work are well known—perhaps even to Milt. However, a leader has to feel when he or she is in step with another person because attempts to manipulate coworkers by posturing may result in initial success but eventual failure. When attention succeeds, it not only provides critical information for establishing trust and resolving business issues but also sets the stage for empathy.

"I See It Your Way": Empathy

In technical terms, empathy is a temporary and partial abandoning of one's own usual personality traits and habits in the service of identifying with someone else's perspective. But why on earth would a leader in a business setting find total immersion in someone else's life a desirable skill? What possible role could identifying completely with a coworker play in the profitability and welfare of the total organization? How does a manager's concern about people's careers, their future, their families, their job anxieties relate to the workplace?

In business, there is a conflict between the good of the organization and the good of the individual. The paradox is that they are both intimately tied together and yet in conflict too. Most often, the pressure from larger organizational goals overwhelms individual needs. Milt's concerns about his management proficiency and flagging business profits caused him to completely ignore his most important resource—Leslie. Most leaders now know that people and their feelings are critical factors for business success, but they don't exactly know how to strike a balance between being "personal" and being "corporate." Empathy holds the secret to this puzzle. In particular, empathic skills rely on one vital quality—balance, a balance between being a full participant and an objective observer of a relationship. By partially and temporarily identifying with another person's world view, leaders fulfill the most basic criteria for a ensuring a trusting relationship, while pursuing critical business agendas at the same time. But what constitutes empathic behavior at a practical level?

To become an agent for changing relationships, the effective leader must be able to demonstrate a basic set of qualities that generate trust and growth. Genuineness or congruence between a person's inner thoughts and feelings and external behavior is one ingredient. A subordinate of a "fast track" manager related how her boss confused her: "He constantly told me how well I was doing and how interested he was in my development. He was like a robot. He said all the right things—as if he'd learned them at a course or something. But I didn't 'feel' he was on my side—and he did nothing to prove it either." In other words, empathy is not an activity that can be memorized or packaged and repeated identically for each relationship. It is a one-of-a-kind response for each individual interaction, focusing consistently on the concerns, feelings, and ideas of the other person. The role of the leader is to accurately reflect or mirror these concerns. In the case of Milt and Leslie, Milt could have significantly improved interaction if he had engaged in the following kind of dialogue:

34 • MANAGING TO RELATE

MILT: Leslie, before we review where we are in the project, I'd like to take some time to hear how things are going for you.
LESLIE: Well, they've been . . . uh . . . OK.
MILT: Hmm, that doesn't sound great. I know you've had a tough time with all the deadlines. How has that been for you?
LESLIE: Well, to tell you the truth, I'm working real hard, but sometimes on the wrong things in the wrong order.
MILT: So we've got some problems with our priorities, eh?
LESLIE: We sure do.
MILT: When you're trying that hard and not getting the results you want, it can get pretty demoralizing too.
LESLIE: Yeah, that's the hardest thing. Everything seems to go wrong; you start to lose your confidence in yourself and everybody else.
MILT: I'll bet that includes me too, eh?
LESLIE: Well, I guess it does.
MILT: Maybe I can help us both do a better job and help you get some of your faith back. Let's spend some time going over exactly where this project is giving us trouble, OK?

By taking just a few minutes to make an emotional connection, Milt would have set a much more collaborative and motivating tone for confronting Leslie's problems and his. Of course, Leslie could have steered the interchange in a more fruitful direction too, by saying, "Milt, before we get started, can I get some things off my chest? I want to tell you about some of the frustrations

I've had, so you can get an accurate picture. That way maybe you can help me see some better ways to improve my performance on this project." If Leslie had initially stopped Milt from rushing into his own ideas about how to run a project, Leslie could have aligned the dialogue to better suit each of their needs.

Empathy supports the health and functioning of human relationships. It is a key factor in maintaining and repairing the interpersonal bonds that underlie all common goals and a quality work environment. Empathy is also one of the most important factors for developing team spirit and positive, ethical cultural values. But as one manager cited, "I avoid being truly interested in others' lives at work. I'm not only not paid for it, I feel punished for it. There's so much pressure for bottom-line results. I get further behind if I take the time to get involved. Besides, in today's world, I might have to fire the people I grow to like." Another more jaded leader rationalized his stance: "I don't worry too much about other people's concerns. When you get into every little problem, when you start legitimizing everyone's point of view, your life is over. People regress and spend all their time bitching and moaning and not doing productive work."

At one level, these managers have a legitimate fear. In some settings, unproductive interactions between workers fulfill their unmet needs for affiliation. Often informal networks that interfere with productivity develop in settings where effective leadership is lacking. This is particularly true where interactive skills are deficient. For instance, in these cases, the problem was probably the leaders' skill deficit. In some instances, they may have closed off subjective feelings and opinions—thus inhibiting mature, creative inputs. At other times, they probably allowed personal lives and personal hurts to predominate dialogue. Both extremes are damaging. The delicate balance based on a temporary and partial identification with another person's wants and needs is the key. Total emotional availability is just as damaging in a business setting as the total exercise of authority.

Subjectively, leaders who are highly skilled at empathy report the internal tensions that accompany their stance. For example, the manager of marketing for a large corporation described how she thinks:

> I often feel confused about how to relate to employees. I can sense that getting closer emotionally helps. So I try to take notes—share some of my own personal concerns and feelings and make sure to hear them out. But getting too close makes work harder for everyone. People start spending more time on each other than on doing the job. So I try to set a kind of limit on involvement, too. If I can stay on the edge of this conflict, work goes well. If I get either too personal or too distant, it doesn't.

How can a leader best reconcile the conflict between organizational demands and individuals' needs to feel understood? Empathy relies basically on an attitude or intention to stay involved with others on a personal level. It requires leaders to tolerate the anxiety that stems from balancing business needs and self-interest against the interests of coworkers. Leaders must demonstrate this stance consistently with behavior that shows a deep moment-to-moment involvement in the world view of the people that he or she is leading. When leader behaviors do not meet these criteria, distrust can grow insidiously among coworkers and undermine effective work processes. When leaders do model empathy, they lay a foundation for trust and honest relationships.

"I'm the Glue": Respect

The best leaders demonstrate an abiding respect for people. They accomplish this mostly through an unconditional, positive attitude for their coworkers that is always present, even in times of turmoil or overt disagreement. A project leader for a leading high-tech firm described how he maintained team spirit: "The software projects I work on are always a rush. It puts a lot of pressure on us for results and it causes heated arguments at times. I often have to lay down the law. Sometimes I even get pretty angry. But I have a rule. No matter how bad things get, you've got to treat people with respect. You've got to hang in there . . . let them know that the relationship is important to you, that it won't get derailed by conflict." This illustrates another aspect of respect—honest, forthright expression of thoughts and feelings. Often, leaders assume respect hinges on being consistently "nice." They fail to realize that giving bad news or voicing an unpopular opinion shows confidence in the solidity of a relationship. It proves the listener is able to be treated in a collaborative, honest manner.

The best leaders combine attention and empathy with respect to consolidate feelings of trust. Respect is primarily demonstrated through open interest in the perspective of others and a consistently nonjudgmental stance. Our research shows that coworkers feel respected when leaders judiciously use the following group of behaviors:

- Validating the ideas and feelings of others;
- Responding honestly to others' questions and opinions;

- Explaining how activities benefit others.
- Showing a willingness to compromise;
- Suspending judgment during conversation.

For example, Milt could have overcome many of his problems with Leslie if he had validated his perception that Leslie was not with them on the project. He could have said something like, "Leslie, if I seem so unavailable to you there must be something wrong. We'd better find out why you feel that way." In addition, honesty must be complemented by the softer behaviors of other interaction skills. Milt's honesty came across as both judgmental and callous because his comments about regressing co-workers (although a legitimate concern) were not tempered by attentiveness and empathy. Instead, he could have responded to Leslie's concerns about not getting a hearing about problems by saying, "I think I know about the problems we face. But sometimes I come across as too quick because I have a bias against getting too caught up in personal stuff, so I tend to stick to what I think is the important business and then move on to other things that need to get done. Maybe I need to slow down in this case. So tell me: What am I missing?"

Perhaps most important, respect serves to maintain the trust bond—particularly during crises and disagreements. Ben, a manager of manufacturing in an aerospace business, clarified how he sees the role of respect:

> I came up through the ranks. So I know what the shop floor and production lines are like. As a manager, now I have to deal with business strategies and let other people implement things. But I'm still the glue in the organization. I hold it all together. I do it by staying in touch with all the employees—on

> their level. For example, I run regular 'skip level' meetings where I meet with workers on the line. I tell them what we're doing and why and I answer any questions they ask honestly—no matter how hard it is. This is a difficult thing to do, but it's one of the most important things I do to keep morale up.

Ben understands that respectfulness, supported by a deep commitment to sincerity and honesty, supports a healthy organizational culture. The best leaders believe and demonstrate daily that people's ideas and feelings are their most valued resources. They maintain the importance of people by showing their own high work standards and ethical values—even when it means delivering "bad news."

"Working Together": Rapport

Although attention, empathy, and respect set the stage for solid relationships, rapport is the payoff. It is a mutual connection in which the feelings and goals of two people form a shared agenda. The best leaders build rapport mostly through an abiding presence, frequent affirmation, excellent communication and understanding, and discussion of common concerns. Susan, a project leader of a software development team, was known for her ability to establish solid working relationships:

> Some of my colleagues think I must spend a lot of time building relationships on my team. I don't! I just follow one simple rule—to stay in touch with my coworkers. This means hearing them out frequently. I'm very proactive about this. I try to see them every day. If I can't, I'll call or write a note.

This makes people feel cared about and it avoids surprises for me. And it doesn't take much time. In fact, I think I save time by avoiding problems and misunderstandings.

Susan's presence was part of her own personal leadership style. It also ensured a sense of connection and made coworkers feel that she cared.

Bill, a manager for an East Coast bank, emphasized another dimension of establishing and maintaining rapport. Highlighting the importance of personal expression, he said, "I make a point of showing my interest in my coworkers' tasks and letting them know my side of things. I make sure we look at each other honestly."

Many experts describe the essence of rapport as a presence in which a person remains in touch with another individual on a minute-by-minute basis. Although rapport implies a kind of harmony or agreement, its origins in French—meaning "bring back"—emphasizes its restorative aspect. In other words, rapport requires a reciprocity that entails ongoing checking and rechecking by both individuals to ensure that their common agenda is center stage. In the case of Milt, he failed to establish common ground for agreement, much less make the inevitable midcourse corrections required for maintaining rapport. To establish rapport, perhaps Milt could have conducted a dialogue to establish a common agenda:

MILT: Leslie, you think I don't understand what's important to you on this project. So tell me exactly what you think needs to happen to make things run better.

LESLIE: I think we've been missing deadlines because the goals we have aren't clear enough and because

	we don't set realistic milestones and then track them.
MILT:	You think those are my responsibility?
LESLIE:	Well, yes . . . and no.
MILT:	What's the yes part and the no part?
LESLIE:	I do think you're responsible for making sure things stay on track, but I don't think you should be doing it alone. Everyone on the team is responsible too for making sure goals can get done on time.
MILT:	I agree. I'm the final backstop, but you're right. I do need help. So why don't I tell you what I need to do my part of the job and then you tell me how I can help you do your part? OK?
LESLIE:	OK!
MILT:	Then let's check our understanding to make sure we're on the same wavelength. I want to make sure there are no misunderstandings about what we're both going to do next. Will that get us back on track from your point of view?
LESLIE:	Sure will, but what about down the road? How will we stay on track?
MILT:	I think that should be one of our outcomes—what we've got to do to keep in touch about my needs and yours.

Establishing rapport is the final step in consolidating a trusting relationship. It is the outcome of using all the interaction skills. Each interaction skill is used separately in establishing and maintaining trust, but there is a very general sequence or flow of behaviors from those that demonstrate attention to those that show empathy, respect, and finally rapport. As misunderstandings and new environmental demands occur, a leader often must return to using more attention, empathy and respect along with rapport. Ultimately, however, rapport is required to support inquiry, directive, and strategic influence.

The Interaction Payoff: Building Trust

The four skill areas of interaction—attention, empathy, respect, and rapport—support all other interpersonal and management interventions. They are the foundation. Without their ongoing presence, other aspects of relating are significantly less effective. All information gathering suffers because the openness that comes with trust cannot develop. Inquiry is stifled if a leader fails to learn about the style, tone, themes, and concerns of others that must be confronted when seeking information and must be interpreted when receiving information. John, the manager of a product development team, noted how his sensitivity to team members helped him interpret their input:

> We all work very closely together. I have to know each person's way of thinking. Sarah is pretty dramatic. Everything is presented as a crisis. She is a solid worker, but thinks that way. So you have to tone down what she says or you'd be running around putting out false fires all the time. Sam's just the opposite. He doesn't express himself openly very well. So if he says he's 'a little bit upset,' you know there's something terribly wrong!

Without the information that comes from closeness, work initiatives can become a game of hit-or-miss actions and reactions.

Directive and strategic forms of influence also suffer when trust is lacking. Coworkers will more often see influence techniques as manipulative measures designed to coerce or control them. One employee of a high-level manager, trained at the best of schools in business administration, stated, "Larry goes by the numbers and he'll die by the numbers because he's a heartless son-of-a-bitch. I always feel he's using techniques from some course on behavior modeling—like 'how to motivate the difficult worker.' He forgets I've taken courses too and I can feel when he's not being real with me!"

Because trust ultimately underlies all processes based on mutual benefit, interaction is at the heart of the most basic business interventions. Sometimes, in situations such as counseling, coaching, or team-building, these skills predominate. In other situations, interaction plays a critical supportive role. Only by merging interaction with influence skills can leaders maximize their impact in situations where they may not have complete or even partial direct authority. For instance, feedback requires trust so that people are willing to give an honest appraisal. Brainstorming sessions need the trust of participants in order for them to feel safe enough to share whatever comes to mind with a group of colleagues. Negotiations also require trust to be developed before the factors driving the bargaining are disclosed and before basic positions are taken. In all cases of negotiation, trust binds participants together so they can tolerate misunderstandings and fundamental differences of opinion. People often fail to understand that negotiations are an interpersonal event more than anything else. In other situations, such as directing tasks or managing the implementation phase of a project, interaction skills appear in more muted forms to support influence techniques.

No matter what kind of management intervention

44 • MANAGING TO RELATE

leaders pursue, interaction skills must comprise a significant part of their efforts. They should be a primary focus of an effective leader all the time.

The following three tables summarize how to use interaction skills. Table 2-1 outlines the mix or range of uses and potential abuses of interaction. Table 2-2 illustrates a general sequence of interventions—and sample statements—using interaction skills to develop trust. This is meant as a starting point for forming personalized steps for those circumstances that require building trust. Finally, Table 2-3 outlines an array of competent behaviors. The three figures can be used as suggestions for individualizing interventions or improving personal skills.

Table 2-1: Interaction: Applications and Limitations

Interaction encompasses a set of skills critical for starting and maintaining the trust in relationships required for all successful management interventions. It plays a central part in coaching and counseling roles. Interaction is comprised of the following general interpersonal skills categories:

- *Attention*—the ability to be receptive to a variety of perspectives.
- *Empathy*—the ability to identify clearly with the thoughts, feelings and actions of others (i.e., to "put oneself in someone else's shoes").
- *Respect*—the ability to take an abiding, nonjudgmental stance toward others.
- *Rapport*—the ability to make a firm, ongoing emotional connection with another person.

TOO LITTLE INTERACTION CAN:	TOO MUCH INTERACTION CAN:
• Result in failure to develop trust and respect with coworkers.	• Regress coworkers, focusing them on personal rather than work requirements.
• Allow small crises or conflicts to grow into large problems.	• Intrude on coworkers' private lives and personal space.
• Allow personal distortions and insecurities to interfere with work agendas.	• Play out a leader's inappropriate emotional needs, impairing judgment and interfering with work agendas.
• Undermine inquiry and directive and strategic influence efforts because of lack of appropriate support.	• Weaken or provide distractions from efforts at inquiry and directive or strategic influence.

Table 2-2: Interaction

KEY ACTIONS	EXAMPLE STATEMENTS
1. State the purpose of the interaction to establish rapport by developing a sense of another's perspective.	"I want to spend some time to get a sense of what you are thinking and feeling."
2. Ask for other person's perceptions/ideas/feelings.	"What do you think/feel about . . . ?"
3. Listen attentively; avoid distractions.	(Arrange quiet space; sit quietly; don't interrupt.)
4. Allow or encourage other persons to elaborate their perspective without judgments or opinions.	"Uh huh . . . OK . . . Yes . . . Tell me more."
5. Express genuine interest/ affirmation about the other person's point of view.	"That's interesting. Great! It's important that I hear your ideas."
6. Check your understanding intermittently.	"Let me see if I am understanding you. You mean that . . . "
7. Demonstrate your understanding by summarizing the other person's feeling/ideas.	"So let's summarize what we have talked about. I heard you say three things . . . "

Table 2-3: Interaction Strategies

ATTENTION
- Make frequent contact with others to keep relationships on track.
- Remain receptive to any input from others; avoid premature judgments.
- Listen for feelings or concerns that underlie the manifest content of conversations.
- Understand and confront your own interpersonal vulnerabilities and limitations and how they affect others.

EMPATHY
- Focus on the feelings and perceptions of others.
- Put yourself in the position/perspective of others.
- Emphasize subjective over objective data.
- Accept and explore the multiple perspectives that people have for each problem or situation.
- Tolerate anxiety or difficult feelings without withdrawing from relationships.

RESPECT
- Demonstrate high standards and ethical values.
- Act in a sincere, honest manner, even if it means giving "bad news."
- Solicit and honor others' perspectives.
- Focus on the value of people's ideas, perspectives, and feelings.

RAPPORT
- Define and tolerate people's idiosyncracies, vulnerabilities, limitations.
- Remain open to the opinions and feelings of others.
- Affirm others' points of view frequently.
- Express interest and genuine warmth toward others.
- Focus on investing your full attention in conversations and interactions.

3

Inquiry

Inquiry is a set of skills for situations that require information-gathering, clarifying ideas, or making diagnostic interpretations. Based on a reflective stance and a focus on tasks or ideas, inquiry is at the heart of every process that demands investigating facts, concepts, or perceptions.

"There's More to Listening than Meets the Ears"

Tom was looking forward to the briefing about plans to improve inventory control with Bill, his manager. Tom arrived on time and stepped briskly through Bill's open door. Bill was on the phone. He quickly waved his hand, offering Tom a seat, but continued the phone conversation. After about five minutes, he hung up and said, "What can I do for you?"

Tom, a bit put off because he thought that they had a scheduled meeting, replied, "Oh . . . uh . . . I thought we had an appointment to work out the inventory problem."

"Oh, yeah. Of course. Let's get to it. I'm all ears!" Bill said. He leaned forward, folded his arms on his desk, and looked intently at Tom.

Tom thought, "*Now* this guy's paying attention—no

distractions, nice body language." Tom quickly outlined each step he'd devised to improve efficiency.

Bill was listening—or was he? Slowly Tom began to feel anxious. His boss wasn't making a sound and wasn't moving; Bill's gaze had become fixed . . . and a little glazed. It was quite disconcerting, in fact, and Tom found his mind wandering as he spoke. He tried to ignore his misgivings, but became even more distressed when he noticed that Bill wasn't quite making eye contact. Bill seemed to be looking at Tom's left ear.

Tom thought, "Maybe I cut myself shaving or something. What's he looking at?" Now Tom was totally distracted. He just mouthed his words. All he could think of was saying something outrageous to see if Bill was really there, such as, "We'll use three orangutans on every shift to run the computers." He resisted this impulse.

Suddenly, Bill interrupted, "Hm . . . by the way . . . where's that memo about the lost parts?"

"Uh . . . I . . . I haven't written it. I wanted to share my suggestions with you first."

Bill was quick to reply. "Oh, yes . . . and the ideas you've come up with are great. I mean, really great—but . . ."

Tom thought to himself, "I just hate it when someone gives you 10,000 ways they really love what you're doing, and then say, *but*!"

"But . . .," Bill continued, "We've got to put some pressure on the stock room workers." His message was delivered in a clipped, staccato manner; his eyes quickly glanced at his watch and then at some papers on his desk.

Tom pushed on like a trooper, "I agree, but I was thinking . . . it's got to be a team effort . . . one in which everyone gets a personal payoff. Right?"

Bill gave a cursory nod but was now fidgeting with a pencil; not much, but enough to be noticeable. His eyes were darting and he was shifting in his chair.

Tom made another attempt to clarify what to do next. "So about those lost parts, I do have some ideas . . ."

Bill interjected as he rose from his chair and put on his coat, "And I'm sure they're great. Let's discuss them at the next team meeting."

Tom assumed Bill was cold from the excessive air conditioning so he continued to expand on some of his thoughts as Bill proceeded to straighten the papers on his desk and finally pick up his briefcase.

Then Bill turned to Tom, standing directly in front of him. Tom waited, assuming Bill was about to say something thoughtful. Then Bill said, "I guess by now you've gotten the idea that I'm leaving."

Tom was barely able to mouth an "OK" before Bill had wheeled and was out the door.

Bill was obviously a poor listener, but this true case illustrates a set of behaviors that are embarrassingly common. He was in a hurry, but everyone in today's business arena is pushed hard by inevitable deadlines and personal ambitions. So how can leaders contend with the constant pressure to act in ways that have a quick effect on the bottom line? In the United States management generally has had an action-oriented bias, adopting the philosophy that aggressive, bold action based on best initial ideas produces best results. In contrast, many other cultures, such as the Japanese, employ more initial inquiry into proposals, concerns, and potential problems. American managers are realizing that exploring possibilities and doing more planning in the initial stages of product and process design result in better outcomes. In other words, going slower in the service of inquiry makes faster progress. Ironically, information-gathering takes just a few minutes longer than the typical management-by-action practiced by aspiring leaders. In Bill's case, he failed in each of the four skills of inquiry, including:

- *Listening* because he did not react to Tom in ways that stimulated disclosure;
- *Questioning* because he did not explore, using a variety of information-gathering questions;
- *Clarification* because he did not stimulate or refine Tom's inputs with techniques, such as restating, paraphrasing, or summarizing ideas;
- *Conceptualization* because he did not try to capture the meaning or ramifications of Tom's concerns.

Instead, Bill habitually cut off conversations by his manner and by asking closed-ended questions. He got answers—yes and no answers—but missed the most vital information. Furthermore, he omitted all efforts at refining the information presented to him. Even more worrisome, he set a tone for his relationship with Tom that will make him reluctant to share his ideas or maintain a spirit of exploration on his own.

Inquiry is an ongoing process that grows from a foundation of trust. By using it, the best leaders consistently foster other people's opinions and initiatives. Setting an open tone for individual relationships as well as for whole organizations is a key part of generating and exploring ideas. Developing inquiry as a cultural practice is important for stimulating the creativity of coworkers. Inquiry has a more practical, day-to-day face too. When used for a specific work problem, it helps define the attri-

52 • MANAGING TO RELATE

butes and clarify potential solutions. When applied to planning, inquiry plays a vital role in focusing on appropriate work outcomes and specifying goals.

To determine your own facility with inquiry skills, use the following checklist to rate your strengths and vulnerabilities. Do you

- Accurately reflect others' thoughts and feelings back to them?
- Use silence and pauses effectively to encourage conversation?
- Use open-ended questions to encourage exploration?
- Summarize conversation and key interactions with others?
- Effectively restate parts of conversation to encourage exploration?
- Solicit a wide range of inputs from others?
- Effectively paraphrase others' statements?
- Keep dialogue flowing with nonverbal encouragement (such as a head nod)?
- Clarify ideas, simplifying them into pictures, rules, or simple statements?
- Reframe or interpret ideas to generate new perspectives?

A significant deficit in any of these skills or moderate deficits in several will limit a leader's ability to perform in many business contexts and roles.

"Tune in and Turn on": Listening

Over three-quarters of effective leadership is done by face-to-face communication. More than half of that should be listening. It is a critical tool for information gathering—but it is much more. Listening relies on empathy, inner dialogue, moment-to-moment attention, and an attitude of commitment to connecting with another person. However, it also affirms and extends the closeness and opens relationships to new information. Unfortunately, most people are not only untrained in listening but also burdened by communication overload and isolated by emotional barriers. In fact, over half of what is said becomes forgotten immediately thereafter. And only one-fourth of the important ideas in a conversation are retained after eight hours.

How can a manager stem this tide of information decay and distortion? Mostly by hard work and a respect for the power of inquiry. One upper-level manager of a large manufacturing firm noted how time pressure affected his willingness to listen:

> I don't have time to sit around and talk. I took this course that had "The Nineteen Steps to Strong Listening." My God, I don't even have time to take six steps to get a strong cup of coffee!

Another manager outlined her day-to-day fear of involvement with coworkers:

> My job is to get the work done . . . not to hold hands. I get sick of this 'touchy feely' stuff. I usually know what needs to be done and when I don't—I want input that's quick and to the point.

Still another corporate leader describes some of the innermost listening vulnerabilities:

> Off the record . . . I don't like to listen. I like to talk, take control. It makes me irritable to sit still . . . as if I'm not doing my job. Maybe I'm

afraid someone will think I don't know what's going on or something.

These are typical, if not universal, problems with information-gathering. Personal insecurities, anxieties about involvement, and prejudices about others impair listening and interpreting messages accurately. However, even without a personality transplant, people can improve how they listen. Self-awareness—particularly about negative attitudes and vulnerabilities—is the first step.

A self-inventory is the best start. Focus on how, when, and with whom the following common psychological barriers to listening distort messages:

- Fear of closeness;
- Fear of appearing stupid, passive, vulnerable, uninformed;
- Overreaction to certain personality types, key phrases, or words;
- Tendency to evaluate, criticize, or control.

In tandem with self-consciousness, excellent leaders start any inquiry process by interacting with coworkers in a way that focuses on the concerns and job role of those colleagues.

This is not an easy or comfortable task. It usually requires that leaders put their opinions on hold and take the perspective of someone else. This state of mind helps them interpret the intent of spoken messages and avoid the trap of attributing their own special meaning to what is said.

A senior executive described the problems he encountered with his first empathic listening experience:

> I just sat there thinking about the other guy's life. I concentrated on what he was saying . . . I mean *really* saying. It made me nervous; it made me worried about him; it made me feel exhausted. I wanted to interrupt and then I wanted to run out of the room. No wonder I have trouble listening; it's a lot harder than I thought.

This internal state characteristic of helping roles—called "sitting with feelings"—gives the listener a clear picture of the subjective mind set of the speaker. The best listeners understand that a mild sense of uneasiness is an important sign that they're really listening, and is not a feeling to avoid.

Listening also requires self-directed effort. But it's much more than just will power. Clear perception relies on clear, structured thinking and specific behaviors. Speaking occurs at about 125 to 250 words per minute. Because cognitive processes occur many times faster, every person's mind fills in the extra space—with fantasies, daydreams, prejudices, ruminations, obsessions, even music. Have you ever noticed you sometimes were carrying a tune you heard on the radio in your head behind your conscious thoughts?

By focusing on a specific, purposeful evaluation of the speaker's intentions, a listener can markedly increase understanding. For example, excellent listeners consciously compare the verbal message with secondary channels of communication, such as voice tone, inflection, unusual choice of words, and body langue. Body language and speaking style are often more accurate indicators of hidden feelings than words. The best listeners also anticipate the direction that the speaker will take, sharpening the focus on each unfolding thought and how it fits with previous thoughts. Furthermore, they test key ideas or concepts and translate them into their own language. For example, one leader, relating how he improved his listening skills, said, "I used to try harder and harder to pay attention to exactly what people told me, but it didn't work. My mind would drift. So I decided to try something a little more active. Now I stay quiet, ask a question or two, and then try to restate how I understand what was said in a few words—so I don't interrupt too much. Then when I know I have it right, I do the same thing over again. That way I'm more involved, more alert, and I make sure I'm understanding things." This or any other method that sharpens listening not only helps synthesize important facts but also avoids the distortions that result from false arguments, exaggerations, cliches, distracting details, and verbal sloppiness or facileness.

Many excellent listeners also conduct an inner dialogue with themselves to help them focus attention quietly. A middle manager of a fast food chain summarized the beneficial effects of this interpretive process:

> "I used to interrupt a lot to get my point across. Now it feels like I'm participating and listening at the same time. I'm more relaxed, my verbal input is clearer, and my colleagues tell me more. A real win-win situation.

Of course, listening is a two-way interchange—a process supported by complex verbal and nonverbal behaviors. Some body cues, such as still hands and arms, augment a listener's receptive stance. Others, such as nodding the head, reinforce the speaker to continue talking. Along with nonverbal behaviors, people complement the listening process by the way they speak. For example, an irritable or urgent voice tone or frequent interruptions inhibit dialogue. On the other hand, a warm voice tone invites further disclosure. As a complement to quiet listening, the quality and quantity of the speaker's output can be increased by the following kinds of behaviors:

- Using short, specific statements or questions;
- Delaying the time between a response and a coworker's statement;
- Making fewer statements; letting the other person do most of the talking;
- Staying on the topic being discussed (or if the subject needs to be changed, trying to do it in small steps that are clearly linked to previously discussed items);
- Trying to match verbal input to the other person's talking style (such as voice tone, intensity, rate, and pauses).

In every case, the selection of tactics must evolve as a genuine response to an unfolding interpersonal interaction. Bill, Tom's manager, could have solidified their relationship while he explored the plans for inventory control if he had conducted the following kind of dialogue:

BILL: The inventory problem. Let's get to it, I'm all ears.
TOM: Well, we knew our costs were too high, but we don't know exactly why.
BILL: (Nods his head up and down slowly without saying anything).
TOM: I did some leg work to find out more about what parts we're using and at what rate, so we can get an idea of what we've got to have on hand and what we don't.

BILL: OK. What did you find?
TOM: We need about half of the parts we have in inventory. The rest are just sitting there taking up space and costing us money.
BILL: Hmm . . . (Bill raised his eyebrows, nodded his head again, and then remained silent.)
TOM: So . . . I think we can significantly reduce inventory, but we have to change some things, like our inventory control system and the way we organize, pack, and store parts.
BILL: When you say we have to change some things, do you mean the computer system?
TOM: Yes, definitely. It has to be much more comprehensive—to give data about inventory levels and to track parts from the loading dock to the manufacturing line. (As Tom became more animated about his recommendations, Bill slowly moved forward in his chair and leaned toward Tom.)
BILL: You mentioned organizing, packing, and storing parts too. How exactly can we improve those too?

The companion to quiet attentiveness is verbal encouragement. It is a cross between checking in and cheerleading that stimulates conversation without interjecting opinion. The most effective forms of verbal encouragement include the following:

- *Acknowledging sounds.* Listen to a normal conversation between people—grunts, single syllables, subtle sounds are numerous. These act as powerful rewards or punishments in daily conversation. When leaders use conscious restraint from making specific comments, (particularly early in the discussion) and instead use selective acknowledging sounds such as "Uh, Huh, Oh, Mmm, Ahh, Huh!", coworkers know they're listening. Intervening in a restrained way encourages dialogue and avoids steering conversation away from coworkers' thoughts and concerns. In Bill's "improved" listening, he used "OK" and "Hmm" to encourage without derailing Tom's explanation.

- *General positive reinforcers.* Leaders often feel uncomfortable giving direct praise. The most simple form—the short, reinforcing comments during normal conversation—works to maintain emotional contact and encourage conversation about the subject immediately preceding a statement. Some typical positive reinforcers include: "That's good"; "I like that": "I need that kind of information."
- *Repetition or restatement.* The repetition of words or key phrases also encourages conversation, when used selectively to focus on key points in conversation. The leader's voice tone and emphasis and choice of words or phrases is a *gentle form of request* for further elaboration of a specific subject. For example, the "improved" Bill restated "change some things" to refer to the inventory system and later also repeated Tom's words "organizing, packing, and storing parts." This action strongly encouraged dialogue pertinent to those practical and potentially productive topics.
- *Direct requests.* One of the most frequently used forms of verbal encouragement is the direct request for information (such as "tell me . . ."; "I want . . ."; "Let's get more specific . . ."). They have several important functions for leaders:
  - To specify areas to discuss;
  - To orient others to their thoughts and feelings;

- To exercise appropriate control over a wandering conversation.

To be effective, all forms of encouragement must be balanced with silence and tailored to a leader's own personality and the individual needs of the speaker.

Listening also goes beyond dialogue. It has an environmental dimension. Every leader is a host—someone who should arrange for a comfortable communication setting. For example, one employee reported that: "My boss has an open attitude about one-to-one dialogue. Unfortunately, he also has an open door, an open phone, an open desk, and an open mouth." It does little good for leaders to be attentive listeners if they don't protect conversations from distractions and interruptions. In contrast, treating coworkers like honored guests sets the stage for effective interchange.

One of the most grievous leadership flaws is overlistening—a rigid, artificial effort that ultimately conveys falseness and fatigues the listener. Quality relating means give and take, silence and dialogue; informal time, and time for focused honest expression. Above all other goals, a skilled leader must be an authentic participant in relationships with coworkers.

Here are some typical comments from leaders about how they reconciled the conflict between their own personality traits and the attributes of the ideal listener:

> I'm basically an impatient person. So I struggle to shut up. When I can't keep quiet, I tell my coworkers they'd better speak up because I've got a problem listening.
>
> I found I had to have a special room for listening—no phone, no papers, and a locked door.

I developed my own technique: Take notes and check out my understanding about every five minutes. That way I can keep quiet and stay in touch.

"What, Why, and How?": Questioning

Asking questions is the primary method for generating information in inquiry. In addition, questions offer a nonintrusive means of "checking in" with coworkers, peers, and managers. Even though questioning serves two powerful functions—information gathering and making and maintaining an emotional connection—most people make too many statements and ask too few questions.

First, asking questions entails not only the words that a person says but also the attitude of the person toward discovering answers collaboratively with coworkers. The timing, intensity, and the type of question each have profound effects. For example, the following dialogue recaps a recent discussion I had with a person who shall remain unnamed to protect the guilty and my good standing with my relatives:

RELATIVE: How was your trip? I'll bet it was very enjoyable wasn't it?
AUTHOR: Well, no. [I had a headache for two days and the meeting with the client was very intense and charged with problems.]
RELATIVE: Were you in New York?
AUTHOR: Well, no. [I was in Philadelphia.]
RELATIVE: Did you get a chance to show them the new interpersonal skills inventory?
AUTHOR: Well, not exactly. [I showed them the "old" inventory because I hadn't quite finished the new one.]

RELATIVE: Then are you goint to get that contract anyway?
AUTHOR: Well, no. [I'm going to get a bigger, more challenging and profitable contract on something more vital to the client.]
RELATIVE: Too bad things turned out so badly.

Unfortunately, closing off channels of communication by using rhetorical or close-ended questions (i.e., those with yes or no answers) is too common in every aspect of life. For instance, how many times at work have you heard a question that was really an accusation, such as, "How could you have done that?" And how many times have you heard questions that are telling you something rather than asking, such as, "Shouldn't you check on that order?" These are typical abuses of inquiry. But what are the different kinds of appropriate questions, and when should they be used?

Closed questions can be answered with a yes or no or with a simple, specific, factual statement. They include inquiries such as

- "Did you . . . ?"
- "Are you . . . ?"
- "Can you . . . ?"
- "Do you . . . ?"
- "How many . . . ?"
- "When are you . . . ?"
- "Where are you . . . ?"

Often this type of question can feel abrupt and may prevent an open exploration of problems. However, closed questions are very appropriate for many circumstances. They help you focus on specific concerns. They provide information quickly. They also cut off rambling, emotional, or unnecessarily lengthy conversations. These approaches may be used in problem diagnosis or to help a group focus on its tasks or in a crisis situation.

In contrast, open questions cannot be answered in a few words. They require a more involved and involving answer. In other words, they encourage people to talk more openly. In fact, because this type of question requires a more elaborate answer, it is often more difficult to use and produces more anxiety. A leader who asks coworkers open questions often unintentionally stimulates anxiety. In moderate doses this can be useful to stimulate involvement and creative thinking. But leaders need to guard against creating too much anxiety, because it can inhibit productive thinking. Open questions include inquiries such as

- "What happened . . . ?" *What* questions tend to focus the conversation on events.
- "How can we do this . . . ?" *How* questions tend to focus discussion on the process/sequence of doing things.
- "Why did you . . . ?" *Why* questions require an explanation. (They can be intrusive and judgmental, if not used carefully.)
- "Could you tell me . . . ?" *Could* questions are usually perceived as gentle and very open, often inviting an overview of a situation.

In a discussion, open questions are usually most appropriate for the initial stages of conversation. This invites a shared responsibility for the diaglogue and gives a clear message about the importance of hearing the thoughts and feelings of the other person. As the discussion progresses, more "demanding" kinds of open questions such as "Why?" or "What are the specific points you want to make?" can clarify options or potential solutions to problems. For example, after Tom told the "improved" Bill that he had gotten some significant information about inventory control, Bill asked him "What did you find?" and later asked, "How exactly can we improve those (i.e., organizing, packing, and storing parts) too?" In the later stages of conversation, closed questions are also quite appropriate to produce a specific mutually understood agreement.

Questions serve several vital functions: they demonstrate ongoing interest in relating; they provide a flexible means of gathering information; and they offer a method for specifying the range, scope, and details of problems and possibilities. However, questions must be coupled with conceptualizing and clarifying to simplify all information gathered into a focus for action.

"Creative Talking": Conceptualization

A mythology surrounds creativity and innovation. They are generally presumed to be gifts or art forms, stemming from innate talents. In fact, most creative business initiatives evolve from an interpersonal dialogue. In personality type, creative individuals tend to be independent, self-directed, self-stimulating, and goal-oriented. Sometimes these qualities appear in people as traits that set them apart from coworkers, such as total immersion in problems. However, the innovativeness of an organization occurs more often through collaborative talking—a particular kind of talking, anchored by conceptualizing skills.

Conceptualization, or the ability to capture the central or most vital meaning of a set of ideas or information, is both an attitude and a set of interchanges with others. Although the mystique of conceptual thinking is that of the "sloppy genius," most conceptualizing thrives on a tension between divergent exploring and methodical organizing. The internal dialogue of someone who is conceptualizing draws on fantasy, half-thoughts, images, dreams, slips of the tongue, and other myriad ways that the mind reconfigures concepts. For example, one young engineer described having three-dimensional dreams in color in which he would rotate figures to try out new ways of designing parts. Another conceptualizer in a consulting business got many of her best ideas while swimming laps or running. Whether she was experiencing endorphin highs or not, she found that the isolation and relaxation allowed her fantasies to flow much more freely. Most of her ideas she labeled "hairbrained," but a few she found very simple and clearheaded. Although internal, self-directed thinking provides the fuel for new ways of looking at what to do and say, an external conceptualizing dialogue follows an organized process. It has two main functions: to generate new perspectives and to crystallize ideas into simple concepts. Rather than a leap of brilliance that results in a completely new and elegant formulation, the interpersonal exchange usually starts by openly expressing reactions to the ideas of others. This takes self-esteem and guts. For example, the head of an ad agency discussed her role in creating new ideas in the following way: "I think people try to decide on the right approach to things too quickly. My role is mainly to stimulate dialogue, to expand the range of discussion, to challenge viewpoints. That forces people not to close off their thinking prematurely. It widens the number of ideas considered. This is a very important step toward eventually developing clear, simple, exciting ideas." In the case of

Bill, he could have validated Tom's efforts and stimulated an even broader perspective if he had augmented the dialogue with some of his own ideas. For instance, when Tom started discussing the use of computers in inventory control, he might have said something such as, "What about putting computer terminals on the manufacturing line, so people could track parts and give feedback about the part they need?" or "Can we use something like those product codes and a scanner to enter data into the system?" These types of input are not intended to be correct or prescriptive but to create new information through dialogue.

Although idea generation fuels creativity, thoughts and impressions must be translated into practical initiatives. Thus, conceptualization also entails "packaging" or simplifying ideas into useful, often memorable, concepts. Sometimes simplifying is accomplished by developing a metaphor, a picture, a model, an acronym to symbolize or reflect the essence of an idea. For example, Bill might have simplified the discussion about inventory control by putting it into the framework or "just-in-time" practices, in which parts are provided as needed in manufacturing—each step depending on completion of the preceding step for appropriate materials.

Sometimes conceptualizing occurs through reframing an idea into a different perspective or interpreting what something means or what it does. An engineering design expert was asked how to improve the efficiency of machinery that makes the glass stems in which light bulb filaments are embedded. After lengthy technical discussions with numerous experts about different ways of "rolling" thin strands of glass in a way to form a rounded end for the filaments, he said, "What is the shape you want?

Hmm, it looks like someone 'pinched' the glass. Why don't you make a 'pinching machine' rather than a rolling machine?" So, they did.

Inventiveness usually does not reside primarily in one person. Instead, a leader's responsibility is to stimulate conceptual thinking by repeatedly evoking new ways of looking at information. For example, a leader of a product design team highlighted how she shaped new ideas:

> I have a team in which everyone else has more technical knowledge than I do. I have to respect that but also get the best out of my coworkers. My main role is to shape ideas. I mostly try to reflect things back to the team—but in new ways. Sometimes I take part of an idea and focus on what it means to our product. Sometimes I try to shake things up by talking about ideas in a whole new way. Sometimes I focus on what our product can do—for the customer, for the business—rather than what it is.

This leader shows how to overcome the most significant barriers to excellent conceptualization. She sees creative thinking as a shared agenda and primarily ensures it by relying on persistent effort, alertness to different ways of thinking, and testing of ideas.

Conceptualizers create information. They not only generate ideas but also develop them over time, making numerous small adjustments as problems and new possibilities unfold. Most important, this process should take place in a dialogue in which the leader repeatedly expands and simplifies ideas, drawing others into a dialogue that generates, adapts, modifies, revises, and organizes information.

"Focusing on Options": Clarification

One of the main purposes of management is to get work done. This goal provides a focus for action. All the communication skills described thus far help with this goal. Nevertheless, leaders frequently fail to complete the information-gathering process. Too often people assume that they understand one another and that the remaining steps for planning and task completion will occur. To the contrary, good ideas and hard work are often wasted because of inadequate or absent planning or because of misunderstood or poorly defined goals.

A good leader can make the process of reaching an agreement about purposes, plans, and implementation steps a rewarding and effective experience by using clarification. *Clarification*—or the ability to refine and summarize information into concepts about which a leader and coworker agree—is comprised of a series of carefully orchestrated steps. It is the culmination of a process in which a leader

- Ensures a warm, open relationship in which coworkers feel "heard";
- Helps coworkers attend to the topic being discussed;
- Focuses coworkers on the various characteristics of the topic;
- Helps coworkers acknowledge or specify particular issues being discussed;
- Helps coworkers conceptualize important concepts;
- Reaches agreement with coworkers by comparing their understanding.

Restating or repeating words or phrases exactly as the coworker says them is a simple, nonthreatening technique for specifying issues. Both the selection of the words repeated and the timing, voice tone, and pauses between statements tend to shape the subsequent verbal output of the listener. In fact, restating significantly increases the general level of talking while it helps to focus conversation. It also makes the coworker feel that the leader is interested.

Paraphrasing or stating in your own words the main point or points of another person's discussion is another type of clarifying behavior that lets the other person know exactly what the leader is thinking. Statements such as "I'm hearing that . . . " or "Are you telling me that . . . ?" or "Is it safe to say that . . . ?" start a bridge of understanding between leader and coworker. These statements should be short, nonjudgmental, noninterpretive, and in your own words, mirroring what you think the coworker has just said.

Summarizing is a special form of paraphrasing in which the leader provides an overview of an entire discussion or subject area. It can

- Focus coworkers on conclusions;
- Organize diverse themes into simple statements;
- Help end discussions;
- Set an agenda for the next topic or discussion;
- Link together things said by a variety of people into common themes or concepts.

Summarizing is a more challenging behavior than the previous clarifying skills. It entails not only capturing discussion into a simple overview of discrete statements or steps but also "checking out" to see if you are correct about what you have heard. For example, statements such as "Is that how you see it?" or "Am I hearing you accurately?" promote mutual understanding. Since reaching agreement requires that everyone perceives things in a similar manner, additional interpersonal behaviors are most often needed, including

- Requiring that other participants in the agreement summarize their understanding of its substance;
- Gaining a commitment from participants about what they plan to do as a result of the agreement, when they plan to do it, and how and when appropriate people will be informed about the results of the information-gathering process.

In the case of the "improved" Bill, he paraphrased Tom, commenting, "When you say we have to improve some things, you mean the computer system?" Bill repeated what Tom said but further specified what he thought was important by emphasizing the need to computerize inventory control. This points out a critical aspect of clarification—it can wittingly or unwittingly influence how concepts become formulated. Judiciously done, clarification does not repeat but adds value to the statements of others. In a later part of the conversation with Tom, Bill might have set the stage for further work by summarizing with a statement such as, "You've made it clear that we can reduce inventory and not hurt our manufacturing process. You've also outlined some ideas about how computerizing inventory control might accomplish this. Now we need to get some more information about exactly what a computer system can do and how to go about the next steps. Is that how you see it?" By summarizing in this way, Bill validates Tom's efforts, simplifies what they know and don't know, and outlines next steps.

Clarification is not only the outcome of all four inquiry skills but the method for crystallizing a focus for effective goal setting and action planning. It is the major bridge from the reflective interpersonal skills and the more active skills required for implementing work.

The Inquiry Payoff: Establishing a Focus for Action

Inquiry skills are the closest companions to interaction. They rely on a trusting relationship but move individuals toward more discrete concepts and activities for action. Therefore, inquiry is a vital bridge in business from relationships to productive work initiatives.

Perhaps most alarming is that leaders consistently fail to exercise the complete range of inquiry skills or institute enough steps when exploration or information-gathering is required. Poor listening and inadequate open-ended questioning are endemic (and well-documented) leadership flaws. Failures in conceptualization and clarification of ideas also abound. The current lack of vision and creativity in business stems mostly from a deficit of interpersonal skills. Furthermore, failure to clarify and summarize conversations is a primary source of business inefficiency and misunderstanding. Skillful inquiry is the antidote for these ills. It must be a significant part of any process in which people want to develop a consensus, a definition of problems, or a focus for action.

The following three tables summarize how to develop inquiry skills. Table 3–1 highlights the range of use and the potential problems. Table 3–2 provides a sequence for a generic information-gathering process. It is important to note that because inquiry cannot proceed without trust, the first step in exploration entails establishing a connection. Most often, an initial check-in is enough. However, if uneasiness, confusion, or misunderstandings occur, a leader should spend more time building rapport before continuing the process of inquiry. Finally, Table 3-3 outlines many competent behaviors for information-gathering. They can be used to refine and individualize interventions and to improve personal skills.

Table 3-1: Inquiry: Applications and Limitations

Inquiry develops skills that are useful in information-gathering, problem-solving, or any process, role, or profession where exploring and specifying a focus for action is vital. Although it rests on a foundation of rapport and attentiveness, inquiry is comprised of its own general set of skills:

- *Listening*—the ability to be attentive to others in a way that elicits disclosure;
- *Questioning*—the ability to probe in ways that maximize information gathering;
- *Clarification*—the ability to stimulate and refine the ideas of others by techniques, such as reflection and paraphrasing;
- *Conceptualization*—the ability to summarize interactions or dialogue in a way that captures the central meaning of topics and concerns.

TOO LITTLE INQUIRY CAN:	TOO MUCH INQUIRY CAN:
• Leave important pitfalls undiscovered.	• Be a significant barrier to productive action.
• Result in a deficit of specific information required for planning.	• Generate data and problems that distract or derail productive efforts.
• Cut off creativity, idea generation, and coworkers' initiative.	• Undermine the translation of creative ideas into practical applications.
• Undermine credibility and trust when exploration is is demanded by circumstances.	• Undermine trust when action is demanded by circumstances.

Table 3-2: Inquiry

KEY ACTIONS	EXAMPLE STATEMENTS
1. Discuss the purpose of the interaction (i.e., develop a clear definition of a problem/focus for action).	"I'd like to take the time to make sure we both know what the problem/direction is."
2. Ask a series of open-ended questions (i.e., what, how, why, etc.) to maximize information-gathering.	"What are your thoughts? How are those things important to us? Why should we continue with this project/process?"
3. Encourage other person's responses with body language (e.g., head nod) and verbal cues (e.g., "yes," "uh huh").	"Yes, uh huh, OK." Nod the head. Repeat the last words or most important words of important phrases.
4. Clarify ideas by restating the most important points in the conversation or by reframing them in your own words.	"You think that . . . It sounds like you mean . . . I think you're . . ."
5. Simplify the conversation by summarizing discussion into a few key points.	"It seems that the most important points you're making are . . ."
6. Reach an understanding on a focus by soliciting feedback about key points.	"What would you add or change about how I'm hearing things?"
7. Come to an agreement making sure there is a mutual acknowledgment of understanding.	"Let's see. Are we agreeing that the focus should be . . . ?"

Table 3-3: Inquiry Strategies

LISTENING
- Remain calm, relaxed, and focused when listening.
- Reinforce discussion with nonverbal cues (e.g., a nod of the head).
- Stay on the topic being discussed; avoid distractions.
- Arrange for a quiet, comfortable environment whenever possible.
- Respond to verbal and nonverbal cues to encourage conversation.
- Reflect on others' thoughts and feelings to stimulate discussion.
- Suspend judgment; avoid premature closure of dialogue.
- Keep comments brief and to the point.

QUESTIONING
- Use open-ended questions to start or stimulate discussion or generate new input.
- Use close-ended or factual questions (i.e., those with yes or no answers) to specify or gain agreement.
- Repeat or restate words or phrases to gain clarity.
- Make direct requests for needed information.

CONCEPTUALIZATION
- Simplify concepts by focusing on specific qualities or by using examples or metaphors.
- Reframe ideas in your own words or from a different point of view to generate new perspectives.
- Interpret the meaning or essence of concepts/ideas to sharpen focus.

CLARIFICATION
- Take an inventory of ideas to generate options.
- Explore the range of possibilities before drawing conclusions.
- Repeat or summarize significant ideas discussed to increase mutual understanding and agreement.

4

Directive Influence

Leaders often must be able to play roles in which they select, plan, control, and track technical or practical activities. This requires a set of interpersonal skills—called directive influence—that are action-oriented and focus on objective concerns.

Mis-direction

Robin was worried—and rightfully so. She was put in charge of a six-month project to close down one factory and consolidate manufacturing operations in another plant about thirty miles away. Everyone knew that it needed to be done for the company to stay competitive, but no one liked it—not even Robin. There were hundreds of details, a lot of angry people losing jobs, and a pressing need to get machinery disassembled, transported, reassembled, and working quickly.

About three months into the project, Robin was floundering—over budget and behind schedule. The first-shift foreman, Bernie, was the key man Robin needed for help. Unfortunately, Bernie had a real chip on his shoulder and gave out overtime like lottery tickets every time they were behind schedule. Robin hinted that they had to watch costs. But Bernie, who ate people like Robin for breakfast, was stubborn and set in his ways. Bernie also wanted to do a good job, however; he respected hard work, and he supported the people that worked for him.

Robin was good with the technical stuff. She had PERT charts, and notes with milestones, goals, and deadlines draping the walls of her office. But, she had trouble being direct and hated confrontations. Robin would think, "I'm a nice person. Why is Bernie giving me such a hard time? He's supposed to be on my side!"

Robin decided to plead her case. She approached the foreman saying, "Bernie, we've got to cut some of that overtime."

All Bernie said was, "I've been here 32 years. This is the way we've always done it. Besides it keeps the guys happy and I don't miss deadlines. Don't you think I know what I'm doing after all this time?"

Robin, taken aback by Bernie's outburst, crumpled and replied. "I . . . I'm not questioning your experience. We're just way over budget."

Bernie shot back. "Those budgets are always ridiculous. They get a bunch of bean pushers together, pull numbers out of a hat, and then torture us with them."

Unfortunately, Robin was too passive. She had excellent technical skills but was uncomfortable and a little shy around people. She didn't understand that it's not nice to fail being directive when necessary. Leaders like Robin too often do not specify and track goals or confront poor performance and negative attitudes—in the service of being nice, or democratic, or empowering. Although inappropriate forms of control and coercion erode trust, it is also destructive to good relationships and quality work to provide poor direction. Robin's lack of interpersonal skills was undermining the project and certainly impairing her coworker's effectiveness.

In many business settings, authoritarian Theory X leaders dominate co-workers. Just as often, leaders fail to chart directions, goals, and tasks. The most effective leaders use measured, balanced control of people, policies, practices, and procedures. They are authoritative without being authoritarian. The directive influence skills—organization, advice, confrontation, and coordination—are the key methods by which leaders circumscribe and select activities for action and regulate vital work processes. Robin showed some measure of weakness in each of the four skills:

- *Organization* because she failed to integrate and shape available information into a clear plan;
- *Advice* because she failed to provide Bernie with specific, clear, simple pertinent directions about exactly what Bernie could do to make things better;
- *Confrontation* because she failed to give assertive, corrective input to Bernie about not giving out so much overtime;
- *Tracking* because she failed to coordinate activities adequately.

Like all other interpersonal skills, directive behaviors must be matched to appropriate contexts. Premature direction cuts off inquiry and often destroys trust. For example, a subordinate described how his boss used an inappropriate form of direction in response to his questions: "I try to bring up things going on that don't make sense, that aren't realistic. And he just tells me 'You just do X, and then Y, and then Z.' He's got blinders on. He doesn't want to hear the problems, so he always treats me like I'm a pest or an idiot. So I quit trying to catch the problems. Now I go by the numbers and let him take the fall." This subordinate's comments illustrate how overcontrol eliminates creativity, feedback, and critical revisions in thinking and planning.

In contrast, a deficit of direction can lead to poor implementation because of missed milestones and failed goals. In a computer documentation project, a "nice" manager, like Robin, gently discussed missed deadlines with her coworkers, often several days or even weeks after missing milestones. Because the programmers always had a lot of pressure to meet deadlines on several projects, they often let that manager's work slide. Because the manager did not consistently confront them, they didn't take her deadlines seriously.

Directive influence is, in its best form, an appropriate method for social control—for regulating and for giving boundaries to business activities. But because it requires personal assertiveness, directive influence can be abused easily. Directiveness often becomes a means for taking advantage of power to coerce employees. Leaders are particularly susceptible to this tendency in work settings that reward immediate, visible, bottom-line results to the exclusion of developing people resources. For example, a manager of a consulting group required that his subordinates start work at 8:00 A.M. every morning. This was an odd request, because most of his staff frequently worked into the night and weekends. To emphasize the importance of commitment to work, he posted attendance on a prominent wall. On many days, he even made rounds to see who had arrived, confronting each tardy employee. His initiative toward "efficiency and commitment" had the opposite effect. Coworkers groused behind his back; they covered for one another; they even purposely "lost" attendance sheets.

In contrast, some leaders have trouble expressing demands or appropriately confronting abuses or shoddy performance. This deficit is just as harmful to team spirit and organizational productivity.

When used skillfully, direction supports many requisite interpersonal and organizational functions. It helps leaders conduct discussions that

- Examine ideas realistically;
- Elicit commitments;
- Control activities by forming practical policies and procedures;
- Specify work plans and demands;
- Confront poor performance or work crises.

Use the following short checklist to assess directive influence skills and to determine your strengths and uncover potential vulnerabilities. Do you

- Give bad news in a direct, honest way?
- Skillfully make compromises about differences of opinion?
- Provide frequent, direct, detailed advice to keep things on track?
- Persist in focusing people on results?
- Confront problems head on?
- Effectively warn people about possible negative repercussions of their actions?
- Tell people exactly what you think or want and why?
- Effectively order or organize priorities for others?
- Take charge to get things moving or overcome obstacles?
- Let people know exactly what you expect of them?

A significant deficit in any of these skills or moderate deficits in several will limit your ability to function in many business roles.

"Charting Directions": Organization

Clear ideas, stemming from well-executed inquiry, are needed for successful business activities. Changing these ideas into action and actions into production is the essence of organizational vitality. Directive influence skills are the primary vehicle for translating possibilities into action. They help harness ideas, frame them into practical plans, and initiate productive activities.

Organization is the least action- and task-oriented of the directive influence skills and is the first step for unifying opinions and developing a clear direction. It consists of a set of behaviors that integrate disparate concepts and desires into a direction or plan of action. In practice, the most competent leaders demonstrate organization by:

- Anchoring discussion with a specific demand or focus; often by clarifying steps to complete a specific job;
- Containing their anxiety in pressured business situations even when they may feel pushed for quick results;
- Suspending judgment during discussion;
- Restraining from premature or immediate action when new situations arise;
- Soliciting a wide range of opinions before making plans or decisions;
- Encouraging the expression of ideas, while resisting explicitly positive or negative feedback.

By taking a stance that couples a demand or goal with a review of options, effective leaders can create a healthy tension—one that drives participants in dialogue toward focused actions. For example, after deciding that cost-cutting was a competitive necessity for his business, one leader used the following strategy to start the process: "I told everyone the outcome we had to have to remain profitable—a 20 percent cut in operating costs across the board. After everyone gasped, I asked for suggestions, then for opinions, and then for commitments to a plan. I made sure we didn't get out of step. That kept things going and ensured that we decided on some concrete actions."

Organization without action, instead of action, or in place of required action is inappropriate. Just as often, however, leaders feel a sense of urgency; they think that discussions about possibilities are a waste of time. This stance not only cuts off vital suggestions but also alienates coworkers. In most instances, failed participation stems from a skill deficit. In fact, one of the only professional quarterbacks to call his own plays on the field often asks for suggestions and concerns before deciding on a play. He has only fifteen to twenty seconds for dialogue. In other words, generating possibilities from alternatives need not be a protracted process. Like the quarterback's huddle, the business leader also provides a holding environment for ideas. This might be something as simple as a quiet, attentive moment without distractions. It might be a short, focused meeting to get buy-in for an idea or to gain consensus for an approach to a problem. It might be a series of coaching or performance feedback sessions. Whatever the setting, a leader's behavior and attitude are the primary means for generating input while focusing on directions.

Besides ensuring a protected setting for dialogue, excellent leaders also select and focus diverse ideas into a simple, motivating plan of action. Therefore, a leader must know when and how to elicit commitments too. In order to generate a sense of direction in others, effective organizing leaders

- Provide information, constraints, and concerns that define the context of actions;
- Contribute their own suggestions for scrutiny;
- Evaluate options, giving opinions and expressing concerns about risks, benefits, costs;
- Carry on "what if" conversations to explore the possible ramifications of strategies;
- Develop a unified opinion by selecting a set of activities, reframing suggestions to meet end-user needs, or sponsoring compromise.

In the previous case about cutting costs, the leader announced the outcome that he expected, provided the arena for discussion, and solicited the discussion he needed to reach a plan. He did not make the decision about methods of implementation. These behaviors maintain trust through the leader's honest, active participation, while he "moves" participants toward a commitment to specific actions. For example, Robin should have followed the steps for containing ideas and the steps for getting a buy-in with Bernie and probably her whole project team. She could have diffused Bernie's obstinancy by requesting to hear his objections up front. Furthermore, she probably would have been able to alter Bernie's perspective by persistently—even insistently—moving step by step toward a specific commitment. As a result, she might have been able to develop a contract with Bernie about specific standards, goals, and behaviors before their meeting degenerated into a confrontation.

The process of closing off dialogue is just as important as opening it. In fact, master organizers carefully orchestrate opening and closing strategies. They maintain or generate openness in the service of creativity and empowerment; they close dialogue to prevent diversions and "wheel spinning" ruminations and to move projects and processes into action.

The final part of closing off discussion is gaining commitment to action. This aspect of the organization process relies on a "structured dialogue" that is guided but not controlled by a leader. The result is a plan comprised of realistic goals, timelines, responsibilities, and actions. To ensure this process, effective leaders

- Maintain a focus on results with co-workers;
- Specify or restate the details of requirements, concerns, deadlines, resources, etc;
- Translate suggested actions with "objective measures" or "accomplishments" that represent an excellent result;
- Define and simplify discrete goals according to the criteria for excellent goals that have the following characteristics:
- Easy to understand;
- Simply expressed;
- Results-oriented, and not activity-oriented;
- Limited in number and scope;
- Challenging;
- Specific in their description of qualities, quantities, constraints, and costs;
- Time-bound with specific deadlines and milestones;
- Subject to measurement and feedback.

Each of the behaviors just outlined can be viewed as a step that must be fulfilled creatively and collaboratively. Studies indicate that goals set by coworkers are usually more challenging and more often completed than those specified by leaders. Therefore, the critical skill of leaders is to set the challenge—a challenge that stretches but does not tyrannize the coworker—without completely specifying the path for reaching it. In most cases, high success results from interventions of moderate risk. Therefore, leaders should limit their role to testing goals and helping others structure plans by "chunking" activities into sets of steps with milestones or checkpoints for rewarding successes and for making revisions without a high risk of failure. A sales manager in the pharmaceutical business cited the following approach to making plans collaboratively:

> I used to make inspirational speeches—maybe I still do. But I found that the production of my team improved the most from helping sales reps break things down into small, realistic steps that they were sure they could do and then being consistently assertive in holding them to the contract we made together.

By shaping the process of organization, a leader not only honors and challenges his coworkers with the best plans but also develops a vehicle for effectively controlling work outcomes and output with other forms of directive influence.

"Refining Directions": Advice

Giving advice is done so often and automatically in business settings that many individuals do not understand, much less develop, the factors that make it work the best. Advice, or giving specific recommendations—is a form of directive influence needed to refine plans and action strategies. Again, like other directive skills, both too much and too little advice cause problems. For example, because she feared confrontation, Robin offered no advice to Bernie. Her reluctance to provide Bernie with impressions, opinions, counsel, expertise, or outright demands contributed to their inability to alter their different perspectives about appropriate actions.

In practice, advice can and should take many forms, from suggestion by implication to vigorous, overt demands. Perhaps the best way to illustrate the spectrum of behaviors that a leader can use is to list sample questions and statements from those that are the least controlling to those that are the most. They might include

- How about . . . ?
- Don't you think . . . ?
- I perceive/feel . . .
- I think/understand . . .
- I know . . .
- I wish . . .
- I would like . . .
- You could/might . . .
- You should/ought . . .
- I want . . .
- You will/must . . .

Notice that open-ended questions are less controlling than closed-ended questions. In addition, statements that are more self-referential and feeling-oriented are generally perceived as less suggestive and less controlling. Statements that are other-directed and more action-oriented also are felt as much more directive. The most effective leaders learn how to move along this "gradient of control" depending on the circumstance. In crises or situations with strict time constraints, or when a coworker is reticent or rebellious, a leader should use a more assertive form of advice. When a coworker needs minimal direction or when less control is warranted, a more gentle form of advice can provide input and yet maximize autonomy.

A leader who was masterful at getting results on projects recently told me: "I am seen as someone who isn't very controlling. But it isn't so. I've just learned how to do it without being coercive or unfair or angry. The first thing I try is to throw out some of my ideas and see how someone responds. A lot of times, that's enough to get things unlocked, particularly because I do it a lot. When that happens, people usually think they came up with the idea. If that doesn't work, then I tell them what I think in a direct, sometimes forceful way. That almost always gets a response, partly because I don't do it very often. If that doesn't work and I feel strongly about something, I just tell them it has to be done and I'll take the credit and the responsibility."

Although the way that a leader words advice is important, other factors may play a larger role in how it is perceived and how well it works. For any of the interpersonal skills in which potentially intense feelings are expressed or confronted, nonverbal behaviors can often amplify or even contradict or overrule verbal statements. For this reason leaders must ensure that they avoid mixed messages when giving advice. In the above case, one of the leader's keys to success was his stance with coworkers. He maintained a pleasant, measured, assured, unhurried tone of voice. In Robin's case, her hesitancy when she said, "I . . . I'm not questioning your experience," and her crumpling posture from Bernie's aggressiveness almost certainly evoked a further outburst from Bernie. Robin's unconfident stance in a way said, "If you've got a gripe or some nervousness, go ahead and unload on me. I won't do anything about it."

Along with the stance a leader takes, helpful advice also depends on how well it is focused. In business situations, the most important rule about circumscribing recommendations is to keep them simple and behavioral—not personal. This avoids the mistake made in the joke about the unsympathetic therapist:

DISGRUNTLED CLIENT: I don't think this therapy is going well. Why am I not getting any better?
UNFOCUSED THERAPIST: You're a difficult patient. You don't work hard enough; you don't tolerate frustration; and you don't follow up on what you learn.
DISGRUNTLED CLIENT: I'd like another opinion!
UNFOCUSED THERAPIST: And you're ugly too!

Although mean-spirited, the joke points out a very typical human trait—the tendency to become overly emotional and broadly critical in the presence of negative or challenging feelings. The best leaders avoid this potential pitfall in directive interchanges by focusing advice on a very limited number of behaviors or ideas. For example, Robin could have been more effective with Bernie if she had conducted the following kind of dialogue:

ROBIN: Bernie, we've got to cut some of the overtime.
BERNIE: I've been here thirty-two years. This is the way we've always done it. Besides it keeps the guys happy and I don't miss deadlines. Don't you think I know what I'm doing after all this time?
ROBIN: I know you're trying to do a good job. But, times have changed. We can't compete on cost if we don't cut back on the overtime. So for now, lets just go over one thing—some ways to keep from working on weekends.
BERNIE: I don't see how.
ROBIN: How about catching lags in production earlier in the week? How about reviewing who is having trouble meeting quota? Or seeing if productivity lags at different times of day or with different parts of the assembly process?
BERNIE: I don't know. I think people are working about as hard as they can right now.
ROBIN: Well, I feel we could look into how some cross-training might work.
BERNIE: Hmm, you mean so we could avoid some of the down time and get stacked up with parts of the assembly and don't have enough people who can do that task?
ROBIN: Right!

By offering Bernie some options for solving the overtime problem, by limiting the discussion to overtime on weekends, and by gently persisting with a more assertive way, Robin could have developed an ally in Bernie with only some small but significant changes in her own behavior. In most instances, excellent organization and advice anchor the planning process and initial implementation steps. Sometimes, however, even more assertive methods for directing activities are required.

"Midcourse Corrections": Confrontation

Confrontation—or the ability to provide corrective input to others—often strikes fear in the hearts of both leaders and subordinates. It taps into a well of aggression and anger in every person, often degenerating into loss of control or outright meanness. A manager once said he could never really confront a subordinate because he "remembered how hurt I felt when I was criticized at home for not being able to understand my homework." In business settings, confrontation is a challenging skill because it can so easily become or be perceived as abuse.

Confrontation, more than any other influence skill, depends on trust. A caring relationship is, in fact, a prerequisite. A supervisor working in an aerospace business described how her boss set the stage for confrontation:

> He drives me hard and even corrects me a lot. But it's OK, because I'm positive he respects me. I can tell that he likes me and basically thinks I'm a valuable person. He tells and shows me that. It makes all the difference.

This case example emphasizes how important the context of the relationship is to the effective confrontation. Similarly, the tone and method of confrontation also must be tailored to situational factors. Numerous studies show that confrontation in group settings, where there is little support and structure, is damaging to individuals much more often than in the highly structured settings with strong group norms and values.

Thankfully, confrontation can take many forms—each appropriate for different individuals and situations. It has three principal manifestations:

- Demonstration or modeling of desired behaviors;
- Demands for commitment to established standards, principles, or goals;
- Direct, corrective statements.

Perhaps the most gentle form you can use is openly demonstrating expectations. Like all interpersonal skills, this is a two-way process in which you openly express and model desired work policies and practices and ask others to demonstrate their commitments. Generating a commitment by example is a challenging skill that requires clear, energetic expression backed by action. To show commitment, an effective leader should

- Overtly specify standards of performance;
- Express expectations and priorities clearly and frequently;
- Demonstrate your involvement in policies and plans.

Setting an example in your discussions is often sufficient to guide coworkers' behaviors in a productive direction without invoking a challenging confrontation. Evidence of energetic devotion, personal sacrifice, or willingness to "get into the trenches" with coworkers must accompany the expression of standards or ideals. Commitment without involvement is just ideology; involvement without clear standards of excellence is failed direction. For example, the visions of many political and business leaders become empty pronouncements because they do not model desired values and practices. Ethical improprieties by business leaders and candidates for high office significantly undermine their ability to direct others.

The second type of confrontation—asking for commitment—is effective only when clear goals, values, or plans are understood by coworkers. By reaching agreement on "external" standards of behavior, you can discuss specific expectations with your staff without criticizing directly. A wise leader outlined how he confronts without correcting subordinates:

> Usually people either don't go far enough or go too far when they confront. Most often, you can get across the point about what you want and what isn't being done well by reviewing what you expect. You can focus on the positive and ask for a commitment. That way, you get results without beating on people.

Sometimes, however, direct, corrective confrontation is necessary. Anything else is negligent. For those instances, you need to make sure to

- Control your anger;
- Avoid personal criticism or recriminations;
- Restate standards that have not been met;
- Get acknowlegment or agreement of established standards;
- Focus on behaviors in the coworker that differ from organizational standards;
- Work on one or at most a few differences at a time.
- Reach agreement and make a new contract about corrective actions.

If, for example, Robin and Bernie had decided on a plan for stopping overtime, Robin might have conducted the following dialogue to confront a poor work performance:

ROBIN: Bernie, ever since we cross-trained our workers to deal with the overtime problem, we agreed to move people around when we get behind with the assembly steps, right?

BERNIE: Well, I guess so. But you know Henry and Inez; they hate doing final assembly.

ROBIN: They may not like it, but you and I had a plan and an agreement! When we have gaps to fill and we have the people who are trained to do the work, we have to use them.

BERNIE: OK, OK, OK. I get the message.

ROBIN: So how should we handle this for the next time it comes up?

BERNIE: It won't be a problem. I'll make sure that we use the people we have to avoid getting behind schedule.

ROBIN: Great. And if you can think of some better ways to solve the problem, let's see if we can work them out and put them into play.

Leaders are busy and often allow their coworkers to get into trouble before intervening. Direct confrontation should be a last resort. In most circumstances, if you detect and discuss difficulties early, you can avoid the need for corrective feedback. Although it may be an unpleasant task, confrontation is, unfortunately, a fact of business life. Effective leaders use it judiciously, to reach and maintain standards of excellence.

"Coordinating Excellence": Tracking

Leaders too often assume that goals and the plans those goals encompass will work in their initial form. This is not only misguided and naive but also fails to take into account the turbulent, open-systems environment of today's business settings. New problems and new opportunities make reviewing and updating plans a vital requirement for success. Therefore, to meet milestones and accomplish goals, effective leaders use an interpersonal skill called tracking.

Tracking is a set of behaviors for coordinating outcomes of work efforts and requires that a leader be visible in the workplace. In part, it entails what Tom Peters, who wrote *In Search of Excellence,* calls "management by walking around." A manager of shop operations in a manufacturing facility descibed how he monitored the people and work processes in his setting:

> I make sure I check in with people a lot. How do I do it and not eat up all my time? It doesn't take that much time if you seek people out and ask them how the most important things in their job are going. For example, we were installing some equipment last year. When everyone was really worried about our deadlines, I made sure to show up at change of shifts so I could see everyone and answer any questions. I'd just drop in and stay a few minutes most of the time. Even more important, I gave a message—that I was on their side, that I was with them. This made everyone feel like they were on the same team and it made people keep on top of things. My check-ins helped me be a better manager too because I could take care of most of the problems by coaching about solutions before things became real problems.

Some interpersonal skills are simple behaviors that occur during face-to-face dialogue. But you need a broader perspective in order to maximize your impact on coworkers. In a sense, tracking has as much to do with how you move as what you say. Visibility and openness are the key dimensions in keeping things on track. A manager of a briefing center for a computer company told me:

> I make sure I'm very visible to my staff. I keep my door open most of the time. I walk around to see how everyone is doing; I don't just wait for them to come to me. Sometimes I give people "gifts"—not real gifts, but something maybe more important, like journal articles to help them with their presentations or some thoughts I might write down about ideas they can try out. And I always make sure to ask how they're doing with their goals. Every day I tell myself, "Take the initiative, get out of your office!" That's the hard part. It's so easy to sit back and let things happen to them—and you.

In addition to providing a presence, effective leaders use their contacts to review, revise, reaffirm, and recommit themselves to goals and milestones. In other words, as one excellent leader stated, "Plans and goals are always the basic topic of discussion; I always keep them center stage." An effective leader tracks plans by

- Reviewing and resetting priorities;
- Taking deadlines, milestones, and goals seriously;
- Surfacing conflicts and concerns frequently.

If Robin had specified her expectations and then taken the initiative to discuss the overtime problem at frequent intervals to reaffirm or alter the plans, she would have improved productivity and her relationship with Bernie and the workers on the manufacturing line.

The best leaders offer themselves as a palpable presence. They provide a sense of contact with the problems and processes that are most meaningful to others by restating goals and commitments, by asking for new input, by remembering and revisiting previous concerns, and by real physical availability.

The Directive Influence Payoff: Structuring Activities

Directive influence relies on interaction and inquiry for its effectiveness. Without trust and a focus for action, directiveness is usually perceived as arbitrary or controlling. In contrast, directive influence, exercised in the context of a strong relationship, most often feels supportive and anchoring.

Directive influence is also the companion of strategic influence. Some aspects of directiveness usually come first, such as assigning goals and asking for commitments. However, projects and processes are inevitably altered by changes and problems, requiring leaders to shift intermittently between directive and more subtle forms of influence, labeled "strategic."

In an ideal world, there would be little need for directive influence. Collaborative discussion and agreement about a focus for action would naturally lead to amenable plans. Highly committed individuals would take personal initiative to reach goals and milestones. In the real world, however, directive influence is a critical business skill. It is needed during crises, when time is short, when work is poor or lagging, and for initiating and completing vital phases of work.

The following three tables summarize how to apply directive influence. Table 4–1 outlines the mix or "map" of uses and potential abuses. Table 4-2 presents a general sequence for instituting directive influence. It is important to emphasize that any directive intervention relies on trust and a focus for action. Therefore, the first steps in any effective directive influence effort build on interaction and inquiry skills. When a relationship's foundation is solid, this "reintegration" may be done quickly. When tensions are high or trust is low, the reintegrative steps should be done with more care. Table 4-3 outlines an array of competent behaviors to be used for refining skills—for individualizing interventions or improving personal effectiveness.

Table 4-1: Directive Influence: Applications and Limitations

Directive influence encompasses a set of skills required for starting and finishing projects and processes, solving problems, and meeting crises or rigid task requirements. It requires a trusting relationship and a focus for action to be effective. Directive influence is comprised of the following general interpersonal skills categories:

- *Organization*—the ability to pull together diverse opinions or ideas into a plan, a simple set of steps, or a new direction;
- *Advice*—the ability to give specific recommendations or directions.
- *Confrontation*—the ability to set high standards, fulfill and elicit promises, and challenge poor work performance.
- *Tracking*—the ability to prioritize and guide activities.

(*continued*)

Table 4-1 continued

TOO LITTLE DIRECTIVE INFLUENCE CAN:	TOO MUCH DIRECTIVE INFLUENCE CAN:
• Contribute to a lack of focus or initial direction in work initiatives.	• Undermine the independence and initiative of coworkers.
• Allow work details and problems to expand, causing missed milestones and deadlines.	• Create a negative, authoritarian work environment.
• Allow faulty work practices or inappropriate behaviors to continue or worsen.	• Overcentralize control.
• Result in inappropriate goals or work commitments.	• Cover up the developmental needs of individuals.

Table 4-2: Directive Influence

KEY ACTIONS	EXAMPLE STATEMENTS
1. Discuss the purpose of the interaction to open dialogue (i.e., develop or initiate a plan of action).	"Let's sit down and develop some goals and a solid plan."
2. Ensure that you and your co-worker share a common focus for action.	"First, I'm assuming that we're going to concentrate on making sure . . ."
3. Discuss appropriate goals and milestones.	"What ideas do you have about getting the job done? What goals should be set? What should be the steps and timeline?"

Table 4-2 continued

KEY ACTIONS	EXAMPLE STATEMENTS
4. Contribute information/advice/directions.	"I think it might be best if . . . Why not do it by . . . ? Let's do this first, OK?"
5. Ask for commitments.	"Are you satisfied with the plans? Can we get these things done by the timeline we've set?"
6. Arrange for "check-ins" to track progress.	"When should we meet again and what can I expect by then?"

Table 4-3: Directive Influence Strategies

ORGANIZATION
- Solicit and use a wide range of inputs in making plans.
- Consider multiple points of view before consolidating plans.
- Make compromises selectively to unify opinions, plans, etc.
- Provide an arena for distilling information and making commitments, such as meetings, brainstorming sessions, action planning, tools, etc.
- Carry on "what if" discussions.
- Specify the details for getting work done, such as actions, goals, deadlines, etc.
- Focus on results with coworkers.
- Collaborate with others in setting challenging but realistic goals.
- Initiate suggestions for improvement.

(*continued*)

Table 4-3 continued

ADVICE
- Tailor the degree of directiveness to the requirements of the situation.
- Make sure your concerns, wishes, needs, demands are clearly and simply stated.
- Focus on behaviors, not personality traits.
- Keep discussion limited in time and scope (i.e., discuss only a few items at a time).

CONFRONTATION
- Develop standards of excellence that outline clear performance demands.
- Express expectations and top priorities clearly.
- Demonstrate involvement by direct contact with work settings. (Maintain contact with the "front lines.")
- Set the pace in work settings by energetic devotion to work policies, practices, and goals.
- Challenge work behaviors that vary in quality or ethical values from established standards.

TRACKING
- Provide proactive leadership that confronts problems in an early, decisive manner.
- "Check in" with others frequently to see how things are going.
- Help coworkers prioritize activities.
- Track milestones, deadlines, and goals.
- Arrange for frequent contact with and among coworkers.
- Surface conflicts or concerns openly and early.

5

Strategic Influence

Strategic influence is a set of skills that is both active and very personal. Leaders generally use it to get things done through other people. Strategic influence is most applicable for fostering or completing projects or for any implementation efforts in settings in which a leader does not have direct control over people or resources.

The Influence Masters

Larry was like a TV personality. If he wanted to, he could have passed tissue paper off as dollar bills. People thought he was a sure bet to be an outstanding sales manager. After all, he'd been a top regional salesman before being promoted to regional manager.

Unfortunately, working for Larry was a little like being a contestant on a game show—all day long. The atmosphere was upbeat—a little carnival-like, in fact. And Larry's optimism and sense of vision were stimulating and infectious. Everyone was turned on, feeling like they'd be sure winners if they followed Larry's prescription for success.

But the act wore thin over time, particularly for Hannah, one of his best sales reps. During "Winter Wonder Week"—that exalted, but dreaded year-end push to close sales at any cost and make a big splash—Larry called in Hannah to pump her up.

Hannah knew the routine by now. Hannah entered Larry's office and said, "What's up?"

"What's up? Sales are up. That's what!" Larry responded. He was already on stage. Of course, it was a question whether or not he was ever off stage. He continued, "Sales are up . . . and you're my lead producer. Let me tell you a secret. I've made a commitment to two hundred and fifty orders this week. You're the one I count on to set the pace, to turn the corner."

In the past Hannah would glow from the praise. Now she just glowered. She did feel pumped up, but more from hot air than from inspiration.

"OK, what do you want, Larry?" Hannah asked.

Larry didn't miss a step. "Want, what do I want? You mean, what do we want? We leaders need to stick together."

Hannah intoned, "Larry, how many orders will keep us stuck together?"

"Thirty from you and your people by Thursday," said Larry.

Larry often shared personal secrets to manipulate. He rallied Hannah more times than he could remember with an appeal to be "a winner," "a leader," "a visionary," and more. However, his emotional zeal wasn't backed by a solid relationship, a solid focus, or solid plans. Larry constantly gave positive feedback too. Unfortunately, Hannah began to feel like a guinea pig in a management development experiment. One time, after being blessed by Larry's generic ritual of positive reinforcement, Hannah said, "Larry uses the 3-P approach—praise 'em, pat 'em, and then prod 'em. I feel more like a dog or a cow than his coworker."

Despite Larry's personal successes, he developed significant problems in his new management role because he lacked strategic influence skills. Based on the ability to generate high-quality work output from others by channeling their strongest work motives toward tasks that are beneficial to the organization, strategic influence is comprised of four basic skills—sharing, persuasion, feedback, and empowerment. Larry demonstrated lack of each of these:

- *Sharing* because he failed to provide information about his feelings, motives, or concerns that would win Hannah's support;
- *Persuasion* because he failed to convince Hannah about the need for change with an appeal that Hannah could appreciate;
- *Feedback* because he failed to shape Hannah's behavior and beliefs;
- *Empowerment* because he failed to make Hannah his agent through delegation, development, or transfer of authority.

Charismatic leaders and visionaries are rare, invaluable individuals. Like Larry, they can sell values and ideas as well as products and services. The best ones can help other people reach unimagined potential and extraordinary goals. Often, however, influential leaders manipulate coworkers in the service of their own power motives. Many lack the compassion for people or the respect for team or group accomplishment required for excellence.

The most effective leaders respect the individual, have superior planning and organizing skills, and use a variety of influence strategies that they tailor to the moment-by-moment demands of the situation.

On the surface, it may seem that strategic influence should be easy. But as a coworker of a young, fast-rising manager stated, "My boss is pure bull. He's totally manipulative. I don't even believe him when he's telling the truth."

A wise manager expressed how appropriate measures to manipulate or control others play an important role in strategic influence: "It's telling people what to do in a way they can hear. That means getting their buy-in by forming a relationship with some depth and by appealing to the parts of work that really matter to them. It can be a win-win situation. You get the results you want and your coworkers feel they've done a good job and haven't lost their autonomy."

What was the difference between these two managers cited above? It is no secret that leaders have interests that conflict with the comfort, concerns, and needs of subordinates. Therefore, managers must not act under the pretense that they have no agenda. In other words, influence techniques should deal openly and honestly with desires and motives. In addition, the best influencers pursue their efforts vigorously, energetically, zealously. They plan carefully and believe in their mission deeply. Furthermore, to be truly effective, any strategy that works must concentrate on important business and personal needs at the same time. For example, a young machine operator on a production line highlighted how effective strategic influence works:

> My boss is always patting me on the back, even for the little things I do well. I know he's doing it to get the best work out of me, but I like it just the same because he says only what he means.

The line worker's manager described how he fulfilled the criteria for successful strategic influence:

> You always hear the bad things you do, throughout your life. But people mostly do things right. So I decided to struggle every day to pay attention to my people and all the good things they do and say how good they are out loud. Sure, I think giving positive feedback improves performance. And I want that to happen. That's just the point—I get better work, they get thanked appropriately.

All forms of influence, no matter how nondirective, are basically strategies designed to convince or control. However, in the new workplace, the prerogatives of power have changed. No longer can leaders or managers expect employees to submissively follow orders. More and more, managers are given responsibility for work projects without having direct authority over those projects. Work in which people must collaborate across functions, especially in areas such as sales, marketing, and manufacturing, has increased as the pace of product and process design becomes faster. Today's workers are different too. They have more education and expertise and greater expectations about shared power. In addition, ongoing organizational and personal change are now the norm, not the exception. People who are masters at influence will be tomorrow's leaders.

Strategic influence generates a vital outcome from a business perspective—productive results—and its effectiveness rests on three factors:

1. Coordinating all interpersonal skills into an appropriate map;
2. Appealing primarily to the basic work motives of those people being influenced;
3. Using the setting in which the interaction takes place to enhance impact.

First of all, the research cited in the appendix highlights that strategic influence, more than any of the other interpersonal skills, depends on combining the other skills clusters with a distinct set of behaviors tailored to work motives. In other words for strategic influence to work, it must combine behaviors from all the skill clusters simultaneously. However, interaction, inquiry, and directive influence skills are used only to the degree needed to ensure that the listener is receptive.

Strategic influence is set apart from other interpersonal skills in that it depends much more on the mix or mapping of its composite skills than the sequencing steps or subtle refinements of behavior. For interaction the primary focus is establishing a human bond. This rests mostly on an array of microscopic moment-to-moment refinements or adjustments of behaviors to establish and maintain attachment. For integration and directive influence, which focus on tasks and concepts, sequencing of steps predominate the skill clusters. But strategic influence uses a more encompassing array of behaviors from all interpersonal skill clusters. For example, a high-level leader who was initiating a signficant change in business strategy clarifies the broad scope of behaviors that are necessary:

> I could have laid down the law and told my staff that the business was going to move in a new direction. But that wouldn't work very well. Instead, I made sure to build momentum. I lined up my allies, made sure I had their support. Next, I made a case for change—a simple, clear, but compelling case based on hard facts. Then, and only then, did I start selling my ideas. That required a lot of convincing, reconvincing, and finally getting them to take on the challenges as their own.

Second, effective strategic influence is vitally linked to work motives. The primary agenda for strategic influence is motivating others by bringing their internal resources to bear on external problems. Attachments to work—manifested as motives such as affiliation, creativity, achievement, and power—are much more diverse than attachments in one-on-one relationships. Therefore, instead of nurturing the singular bond between two people, strategic influence requires selecting and nurturing a number of complex attachments to the environment. Some people will be influenced by appeals to team spirit; some by challenging personal goals; some by the promise of innovative, ground-breaking work; some by the opportunity to work with upper-level management.

Third, because strategic influence is much more focused on the ways people are productive, and because people produce results through complex social interchanges, this set of skills depends very much on its social context. So leaders who excel at strategic influence are skillful at manipulating the environment. They concentrate on controlling time, place, and person. One leader described how she timed the presentation of a new idea to coincide with a significant team success. Another leader cited how he used the amenable atmosphere of business lunches for building alliances. Still another highlighted how she often used a team setting where she had supportive colleagues to first introduce new, challenging ideas.

You can determine strengths and uncover vulnerabilities by reviewing the following checklist of behaviors, assessing strategic influence skills. Do you

- Frame things in terms of the benefits of others?
- Dramatize situations to produce a positive impact?
- Reframe ideas into new perspectives?
- Time interventions with others to maximize impact?
- Promise future rewards as a way of fostering desired behavior in the present?
- Give specific, frequent, positive feedback?
- Refer to common values, shared opinions, or principles to convince?
- Demonstrate, model, or illustrate desired behaviors?
- Openly disclose feelings and thoughts to influence others?
- Use logical and emotional appeal to persuade?

A significant deficit in any of these skills or moderate deficits in several will limit a leader's ability to perform in many business contexts and roles.

"Open to Possibilities": Sharing

Sharing—or the open disclosure of feelings, motives, or information to build momentum for specific action—sets the stage for getting others to implement productive business strategies. In its most effective form, it is the heart of mentoring. Sharing fuels action in several ways. It

- Provides necessary information for successful intervention;
- Details potential paths for implementation;
- Structures expectations;
- Models vital feelings, attitudes, and thinking processes that enhance personal productivity.

For example, a young consultant in a management development firm reflected on his boss's methods of supervision, "Jane is a great mentor. She tells me exactly what's going on in her head—even her worries. That's made it much easier for me to get my work done because I know my uncertainties are natural and I've been shown a path that works for getting things done."

Disclosure also has implicit effects. In the setting of a trusting relationship, sharing stimulates identification with the person who reveals information. People naturally tend to try behaviors offered in a clear, open, honest, and confident manner. For example, a wise manager of a human resource department told me, "Mostly, I act as a resource. I initiate telling people about my experiences, my instincts, my impressions. I try to set out a gourmet meal of ideas and then let others select what they want to eat. Usually, that's enough 'nourishment' to move things in a productive direction."

Openness is not only the key to modeling desired behaviors but also improves performance by specifying expectations and activities. All too often, leaders will share simple adages or general prescriptions for solving problems—failing to provide the details that are the essence of their success. For example, a high-level manager of a pharmaceutical firm noted:

> I used to manage by the books. But I never got the results I wanted. At first I thought it was because no one else could follow directions. Then I learned it was because I wasn't following the rules. I found out that I wasn't providing enough information—about what I meant, what I felt, what I sensed. You've got to give the details about what you want and why. Coworkers need to know the details to perform well.

In the typical organization, sharing feelings is shunned. Some studies of managerial effectiveness show that leaders who are forceful, assertive, decisive, and dominating are perceived as more successful. These traits are consistently seen as more valuable than traits such as warmth, compassion, or tenderness. Sharing, which is the natural bridge between interaction skills and the other influence skills, is often avoided or at least not developed because as one manager put it, "It takes up too much time and it's too 'touchy feely' for my job. I've got to stick to business. I'm not running a social club."

In reality, subjective, personal inputs are shared all the time. Not only do individuals express their preferences and worries "off the record," but they "leak" their true feelings constantly through body language and voice tone. Therefore, more purposeful sharing just puts things on the record in a way that prevents distortion and adds the value of a leader's wisdom from experience.

As with all interpersonal skills, sharing is a form of balance—too much and too little are both forms of skill deficit. For instance, I recently greeted a coworker with the polite and perhaps perfunctory, "Good morning. How are you today?" He proceeded to tell me, in detail, about his health, his family, his car, his dog. I was only expecting to touch base, not receive a discourse on the state of his life. In contrast, most leaders sow the seeds of misunderstanding or rebellion by failing to share. By pressing for premature action, they actually slow progress and undermine the confidence and development of their coworkers.

In the case of Larry and Hannah, Larry could have influenced Hannah in a positive way by revealing thoughts and feelings more honestly. He might have conducted a dialogue such as this:

HANNAH: What's up, Larry?
LARRY: I'm hoping sales are up! This is supposed to be our biggest week of the year. I've made a commitment that's really going to stretch us. Two hundred and fifty orders!
HANNAH: That's an awful lot.
LARRY: Here's how I figure it. I'm mostly counting on our regular producers. They got 150 orders last year. I think we can get 20 percent more output if we start lining up our leaders earlier and improve our prizes. I figure we'll get thirty orders from the rest of the reps. I don't think we should concentrate too much special effort there—it doesn't give us enough return in the short run.
HANNAH: Hmm . . . That's a good point. I always spend a lot of time during that week holding people's hands.

LARRY: We need to develop staff, but this is the week to make a splash. The last orders needed, I figure you and I and Marlene can produce if we start now and work our tails off.

By using a dialogue such as this, Larry could have outlined his wishes and his ideas about reaching them and set the stage for other forms of influence, both strategic and directive. Often setting the stage for action provides enough information and stimulation to move a coworker toward more productive action. In this case, with a dramatic demand with a fixed deadline, other directive and strategic influence techniques would almost certainly be required.

"Seeing It my Way—and Yours": Persuasion

Persuasion, or the ability to develop an appeal to the work motives of coworkers, is a key skill for selling anything from a product to an idea or ideal. Too often, it is presented as an art—a mysterious mix of incantations known only to snake oil salesmen and CEOs. Although each strategic influence skill is tailored to the work motives of the listener, persuasion is focused on linking work demands to personal needs or wishes. It translates activities for organizational benefit into activities for personal benefit too. In any sales training, the most vital step toward getting someone to buy is translating the features of your product into benefits for the customer. For instance, in purchasing an automobile, the appeal to a potential buyer may reside in any number of dimensions—cost, quality, reliability, performance, status, aesthetics. Similarly, in other situations where persuasion affects behavior, an effective appeal must be made.

It is important to remember that persuasive techniques

are effective only to the extent that they tap into a personal motive. For example, a middle manager of a financial services firm noted:

> I persuade people by knowing what they want. It's that simple and it's that hard. Most of the effort is in the upfront work of learning what your people are like and what their exact concerns are. Only then can you find the right tack for presenting your case.

An appeal to emotion or ethical principle works best for people who are primarily motivated by affiliation with others. These individuals are more likely to focus on interaction skills as a preferred style of relating. This type of person will often purposefully or unconsciously engage leaders in personal discussions about feelings and opinions or in coaching or counseling sessions. To persuade such individuals, a leader should try to find ways that productive actions by the coworker will promote closer, more secure, more varied, richer, or more esteemed relationships. For example, if Hannah, the sales rep, was strongly motivated by affiliation, Larry might have used some of the following statements to persuade her to make an extra selling effort:

> We've got a good team of people. But reaching our goal is going to consolidate our team with a special sense of esprit.

> This week is going to be hard, but I know you. It's going to give you a real sense of satisfaction helping your people develop.

> I'm counting on you, Hannah. This week will give us a chance to work hand-in-hand. I think we've got a lot to offer one another.

A logical or conceptual appeal works best for people who are motivated by the need to create. These individuals often demonstrate inquiry skills as a preferred relating style. They instinctively question and conceptualize. To persuade these coworkers, a leader should frame an appeal for action by showing how it can offer an opportunity for working with ideas or concepts. To influence the creative side of Hannah, Larry might have used statements such as

> Last year we got a 10 percent bump in sales per rep by using prizes as incentives. How about your looking into how we can design some rewards that might work better—such as money, a vacation, or something?
>
> Hannah, we need some sort of unifying theme—a kind of campaign. Something inspirational to pull this special week together. That's the kind of thing you're good at.

An appeal to standards works best for people motivated by achievement. Because these people often demonstrate directive influence as a preferred interpersonal skill style, they are most comfortable in situations that require planning, goal-setting, or controlling the work of others. To persuade these coworkers, a leader should appeal to the wish to control and perfect outcomes. Larry might have used some of the following statements if Hannah's primary interest was high achievement:

> Hannah, you were my number two producer last year. If you and your reps get those thirty orders, I think you'll win the contest this year.

> If we lay out a system for rating and tracking our customer leads, I'll bet we can increase the number of sales we get per customer call.

An appeal to higher authority or organizational benefit works best for people primarily motivated by power. These people usually prefer strategic influence as an interpersonal style. They are often persuaded most by appeals to status privilege and high impact in the organization. Larry might have used some of the following statements if Hannah's primary interest was power:

> Hannah, I think meeting our goals for this important week might help both of us move up the ladder. I think you're just about ready for a regional manager position.

> Hannah, if your group meets quota, I think you deserve to get first crack at the customer leads in the educational market.

Although knowing what appeals to coworkers is required for persuasion, knowing how to make an appeal is just as important. Some leaders have the natural sales ability or charisma to get their point across. However, most leaders do not come by the persuasive art naturally. Competency studies, which discriminate the behaviors that produce success in any field, have highlighted the attributes of persuasive individuals. Best performers

- Demonstrate honest, ethical behavior consistently;
- Time interactions for maximum impact;
- Maintain an energetic, optimistic stance;
- Refuse to be discouraged or dissuaded when various persuasive techniques fail;
- Focus persistently on the interests of others.

As with all strategic influence skills, the most successful performers use their personalities, the group context, the organizational setting, and timing to bolster impact. For example, a sales rep for a computer manufacturer described part of his sales approach in the following manner:

> I acted in college. There's this concept called "the dramatic moment" when the whole psychology of a play takes a turn in some direction. Selling is like that too. Although you have to know what kind of strategy will appeal to your customer, you also have to have the right build-up of value and sense when to ask for the order.

One of the distinct advantages leaders have in planned events and oppportunities such as meetings, presentations, or coaching sessions is their ability to plan their strategic influence strategies. Leaders can formulate and practice their methods of appeal but also exercise some control over their environment.

Persuasion entails changing another person's mind. A leader must develop both an argument and find flaws or vulnerabilities in already established strategies and plans. For example, experts in negotiation at Harvard Business School have developed a concept called "the best alternative to a negotiated agreement" or BATNA. They emphasize that the essence of negotiation is strengthening one's BATNA and finding ways to answer the BATNA of the opposing person or group.

Persuasion spurs people into action or redirects their efforts, but another strategic influence skill, called feedback, is needed to refine and continue any implementation processes.

"A Rewarding Experience": Feedback

Feedback—or the ability to reinforce, redirect, or sharpen the focus of people's efforts—is one of the most important measures leaders use to influence others. This set of behaviors is demonstrated on a very personal level with interchanges such as "a pat on the back" for a task well done or on a larger scale with accolades or a monetary bonus for reaching significant goals.

Put simply, feedback shapes the behaviors of coworkers through five simple techniques:

1. Rewards;
2. Punishments;
3. Negative feedback;
4. Contingency management;
5. Context manipulation.

Rewards—or a positive reinforcement that occurs after a desired event—is perhaps the most effective and most used form of feedback. You can and should use this type of influence frequently during the natural course of conversations with comments such as "Good," "That's good," "I like that." Rewards can also take a more elaborate form such as a positive report in a performance feedback session. In all its manifestations, however, positive feedback should be simple and direct, should stem from an honest appraisal, and should be close in time to the desired behavior. In addition, a special form of positive reinforcement called "shaping" offers even more power to move coworkers toward productive action. It entails reinforcing only those selective aspects of behavior that most closely resemble specific, desired outcomes.

Without implying that colleagues should "work like

dogs," dog training is an excellent example of the shaping concept. In the process of learning how to heel, a dog is first praised for being dragged with a leash. Then praised only for spontaneously following while on a leash. Then more selectively praised specifically for following and staying adjacent to the owner's left leg. Then even more selectively praised for staying in position with stops and starts and turns. And finally, praised selectively for staying in position during each maneuver without a leash.

The process in business (although some leaders might prefer the "leash and choke collar method") is done through verbal reward for the part of a coworker's behavior that is most desired and selective inattention to behaviors that are less desirable. In addition, like dog training, shaping is a process with multiple small steps, each relying on the continuity stemming from trust.

A project leader in a manufacturing firm illustrates how she used shaping in team meetings:

> I often start things rolling by floating an idea for the team. Then I'm most positive about the responses I think will work on a practical level. Next, I might summarize the suggestions that I feel are best and ask for more input. Then I start the process over again. That way I can get a lot of creative input, make people feel good, and keep things moving in a direction I like all at the same time.

Punishment or unrewarding feedback applied after an undesired event is used too often by leaders. They may implicitly and explicitly criticize or express disappointment about failed efforts. In one sense, this is inevitable—even appropriate, at times. However, theory and practice both share the view that punishment is significantly less effective than reward at producing desired behavior.

Negative feedback—or stopping a punishment when a desired behavior is demonstrated—is another poor tactic. A typical example in a work setting might entail the grumpy or negative boss who brightens only when something extraordinarily special happens. This will make his subordinates try to relieve their pain and his. However, it produces partial results at best. Besides their limited positive impact, punishment and negative feedback also produce undesired long-term effects, such as low self-esteem, covert struggles, and demoralization.

Contingency management, which sets the criteria to be fulfilled before a reward is provided, is a very effective influence technique, although technically it is more a type of "feed-forward" than feedback. In business settings, it is most often used in a bonus system or promising a privilege or position advancement. Or it could be as simple as trading favors.

Manipulating context also can increase desired behaviors. Experience shows that you can enhance the likelihood of particular outcomes by reproducing the setting in which they previously occurred. This "don't-change-a-winning-game" approach to influencing others is too often ignored. Leaders frequently miss opportunities for significant leverage by not noting and reproducing the context of successful interpersonal interchanges.

In the case of Larry and Hannah, Larry could have used several forms of feedback in a dialogue, such as

LARRY: Hannah, what suggestions do you have for meeting quota this week?
HANNAH: How about changing the prizes?

LARRY: Great! How would you do it?
HANNAH: Most of my people want money, not a TV or toaster oven.
LARRY: That's a good thought. What kind of money would make them work harder?
HANNAH: Hmm . . . maybe $20 on an order.
LARRY: Well, I'll make you deal. If you can meet your quota, I'll give you $30 an order for you and your people.

Although each of the five forms of feedback help shape behavior, it is critical to note that these same five techniques are unwittingly used to develop bad work practices and unethical behavior. For example, one inspector on a production line that began producing an inordinate number of faulty parts illustrates how feedback can go awry:

> We get pressure all the time to meet quota. I think my boss gets his bonus on the number of parts we put out. So every time I stop the line because of a defect, he yells at me. I guess I stopped looking for the problems after awhile.

Furthermore, both undesirable and desirable behaviors can be maintained by a process called intermittent reinforcement. This can be a powerful form of leverage because regular, positive input tends to perpetuate the directly rewarded behaviors, even when they are not reinforced, as well as similar kinds of behavior. One project manager reported scheduling regular fifteen-minute updates with his coworkers to ensure that he provided positive feedback. It is important to remember that coworkers can become insensitive to totally positive feedback or relatively continuous rewards. As a result, they tend to counter inappropriate feedback with negative self-assessments.

"People Power": Empowerment

The final and perhaps most difficult type of strategic influence is empowerment—or the process of passing authority or power to others. Although it relies on the related skills of feedback and sharing, empowerment also requires a more direct, mutual, collaborative dialogue.

Frequently, this skill takes the form of delegation. Occasionally, it may be seen as "passing the buck" or simply relinquishing responsibility when turning over tasks results in more work with no personal benefit to the coworkers. The reallocation of a work load is one outcome of empowerment, but the primary interpersonal benefit stems from a fundamental restructuring of the power relationship. It means freely giving power or authority. This activity goes well beyond social manipulation to transferring privileges and responsibilities.

A project leader in charge of a software development effort for an aerospace firm described what empowerment meant for his job:

> I used to use terms like *collaboration, participative management, democratic workplace,* but I didn't really know what they meant, much less how to do them. I was good at delegating tasks, but I kept the power. Now it's different. About a year ago, it became clear that I couldn't keep up with the technologies we were using on the project. I had to rely on my programmer, Bill. I decided I had to trust him, rely on him. And I told him so and let him know he

was responsible for the technical side of the software. Bill liked the idea, until he realized he was on the line too. We both felt uneasy for awhile—I felt insecure about losing control; he felt insecure about having control. Now we talk, share, and fight a lot, but it's OK because we're partners who complement and rely on one another.

Turning over authority also requires a shift in both attitude and practice. It means sharing power and sharing privilege. It means sharing wisdom too. An upper-level leader described how he empowered one of his subordinates:

I was grooming Sarah to move up—to take my place. I didn't say it directly, but I shared a lot of my responsibilities with her. I made sure to give her every opportunity to develop. Some things were formal, such as courses, workshops, access to my network. Other things were informal, such as telling her directly how I do things.

Empowerment also has a demand. It has the expressed expectation that a coworker will take on the mantle of authority responsibly. In the case of Larry, he could have used empowerment with Hannah by holding Hannah responsible for the contest and then supplying Hannah with his input and any needed resources for implementation. By treating Hannah as his "surrogate" he could have changed their power relationship and provided her with a significant growth experience.

The Strategic Influence Payoff: Implementing Through People

Strategic influence is the primary vehicle in today's business setting for getting things done. It includes an array of techniques that are and will become even more the hallmark of effective leaders. Because strategic influence is an indirect form of control and because it rests on a foundation of each of the other three skill areas—interaction, inquiry, and directive influence—it is the most challenging to master. The influence master must learn a wide range of behaviors, must be able to select high impact interventions, and must be able repeatedly to "reintegrate" or rebuild relationships over and over again.

The following three tables summarize how to apply strategic influence. Table 5-1 outlines the range of use and potential abuses. Table 5-2 highlights a general sequence of behaviors for instituting strategic influence. Table 5-3 outlines an array of competent behaviors to be used for individualizing interventions or refining personal skills.

Table 5-1: Strategic Influence: Applications and Limitations

Strategic influence encompasses a set of skills vital for getting things done, particularly in settings of responsibility without full authority. The trust that stems from interaction and the focus from inquiry is required to select the appropriate influence strategies. Moreover, strategic influence is the partner of directive influence—both are required at different phases of projects and processes. Strategic influence is comprised of the following general interpersonal skill categories:

- *Sharing*—the ability to stimulate others' behavior by being open with feelings, motives, interactions, or concerns;
- *Persuasion*—the ability to convince others through appeals to their basic work motives;
- *Feedback*—the ability to shape others' behavior through rewards, confrontation, or expectations;
- *Empowerment*—the ability to get others to implement desired activities by passing authority through delegation, demonstration, or development.

TOO LITTLE STRATEGIC INFLUENCE CAN:	TOO MUCH STRATEGIC INFLUENCE CAN:
• Result in stalled projects and processes from failure to convince, inspire, or empower coworkers.	• Interfere with efforts at establishing trust, gathering information, or making plans.
• Result in lack of commitment or demoralization from too little buy-in.	• Become or seem manipulative.
• Contribute to unfocused or unbridled efforts from a deficit of information or	• Fail to address work problems requiring immediate action
• Result in lack of initiative from failed direction or feedback.	

Table 5-2: Strategic Influence

KEY ACTIONS	EXAMPLE STATEMENTS
1. Discuss the purpose of the interaction to open a dialogue (i.e., to develop strategies or implement action steps).	"Let's work on some practical steps for getting the job done."
2. Ensure that you and your coworker share a common focus for action and clear goals.	"First, why don't we go over what we're planning to do to make sure we agree? What goals should we set and how should we organize steps for meeting them?"
3. Review problems or potential problems with implementation.	"What do you foresee getting in the way of completing our plans?"
4. Offer appropriate suggestions or input (i.e., information, feelings/opinions, logical or emotional appeal, reinforcement).	"In my experience . . . From a logical point of view/to meet your own job needs best, this plan will . . . This part of your plan is excellent; it's really to the point!"
5. Agree on strategies for implementation.	"Let's go over what you're planning, how you're going to implement it and what resources I can provide to help."

Table 5-3 Strategic Influence Strategies

SHARING
- Provide appropriate information openly to shape behavior.
- Admit concerns or confusion.
- Be open about motives, intentions, problems.
- Use self-disclosure to convince or motivate.

PERSUASION
- Use logical explanation to convince.
- Invoke values or principles to shape behavior.
- Present benefits from perspective of others.
- Exhibit optimism or enthusiasm.
- Frame things in terms of common goals/interests.
- Time interventions for maximum impact.

FEEDBACK
- Give bad news or appropriate negative feedback directly.
- Encourage with frequent, positive reinforcement.
- Show appreciation with positive statements.
- Confront situations to coerce or convince.
- Withhold rewards or trade favors to shape behavior.
- Set up expectations of reward to encourage behavior.
- Deflect others' initiatives to suppress conflict.

EMPOWERMENT
- Demonstrate to others how to make an impact. (Model desired behaviors.)
- Transfer authority or resources to act as your agent.
- Give credit frequently and specifically.
- Validate the position/opinions/rights of others.
- Share and compromise with others to get buy-in and commitment.
- Develop the confidence and skills of coworkers.

6

Applying the 4-Is

Fitting Interpersonal Skills to Context

To change a relationship or influence someone else to change can seem like an overwhelming task. As we have seen, a large number of factors affect relationships, so how can you make change happen? Fortunately, small modifications of behavior can make a big difference. By reframing the confusing complexity of interpersonal skills into a simple picture, the 4-I model can help you define small self-improvement projects. (See Figure 6-1.) The model offers a method for focusing on specific behaviors to improve the mix, sequencing, and refinement of skills. Small, consistent behavior change in any of the three dimensions will increase your effectiveness.

The danger of a simple model is losing the essence of the give-and-take and natural flow of relationships. However, a far larger pitfall comes from being so overwhelmed by personal habits and rigid relationship patterns that nothing can be controlled or changed. By focusing on a specific behavior change, you can be more sure of developing applicable skills for business. The 4-I model gives you this means of growing while you face the increasingly competitive challenges of a new, more open work environment.

Fit to Work

Interpersonal skills represent "the necessary, but not sufficient" resources for all effective leadership interventions. With slight variations, every leadership situation can be portrayed as a part or complete representation of a basic cycle. (See Figure 6–2). People use the full range of interpersonal skills most of the time, but different skill maps, sequences, and refinements support or develop various stages of the cycle.

Figure 6–1: 4-I Model of Interpersonal Skills

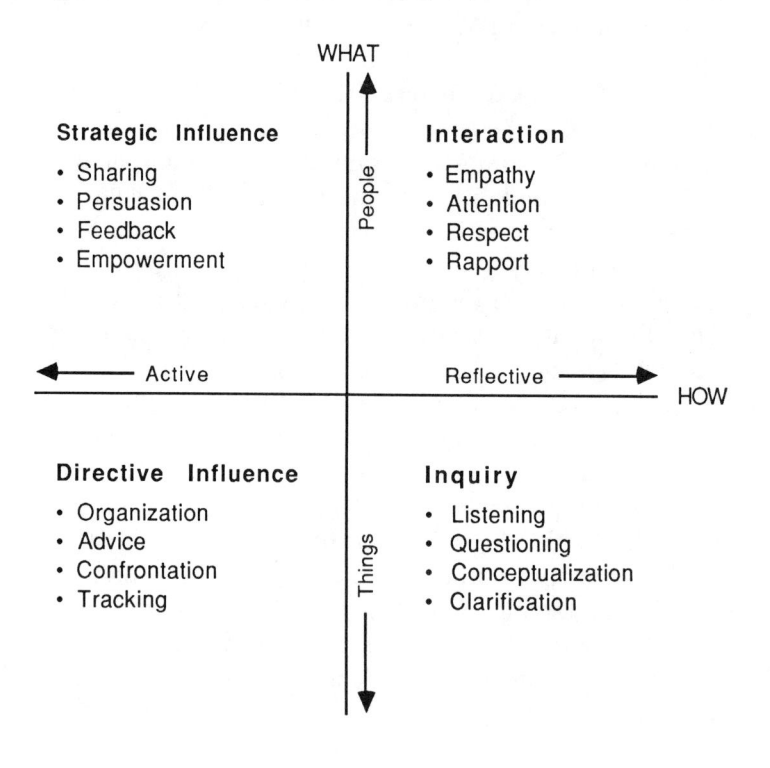

	WHAT (People)	
Strategic Influence • Sharing • Persuasion • Feedback • Empowerment		**Interaction** • Empathy • Attention • Respect • Rapport
← Active		Reflective → HOW
Directive Influence • Organization • Advice • Confrontation • Tracking	Things	**Inquiry** • Listening • Questioning • Conceptualization • Clarification

Applying the 4-Is • 129

The primary consideration in any personal strategy for applying interpersonal skills is the individual relationship with each coworker. At every moment in time, the immediate needs of each relationship should take precedence. This is a daunting task because of the profound pressures caused by situational demands. Nevertheless, the best leaders maintain an unswerving focus on people, while they meet business needs. The 4-I model offers a way to assure connectedness between people during each of the

Figure 6-2: The Management Cycle

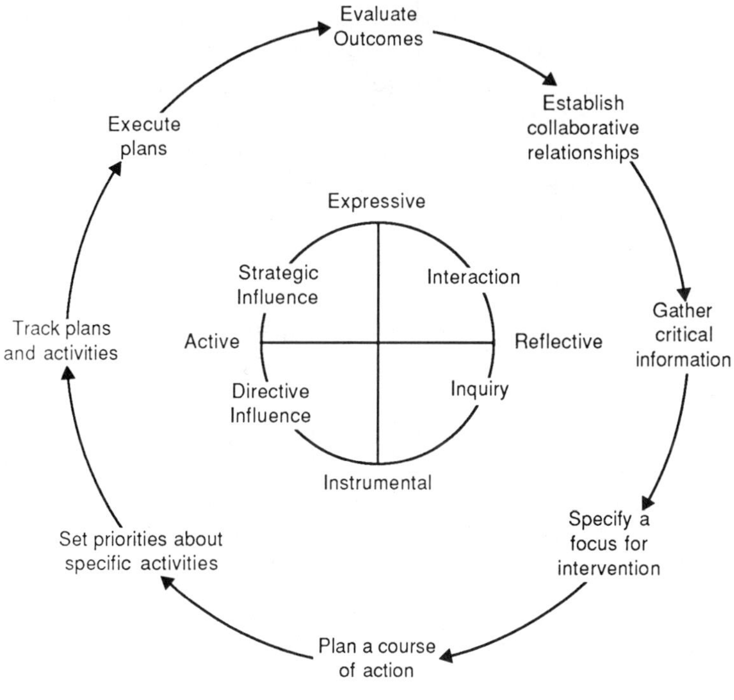

Outer cycle: Evaluate Outcomes → Establish collaborative relationships → Gather critical information → Specify a focus for intervention → Plan a course of action → Set priorities about specific activities → Track plans and activities → Execute plans

Inner quadrants (Active/Reflective × Expressive/Instrumental):
- Strategic Influence (Active-Expressive)
- Interaction (Reflective-Expressive)
- Directive Influence (Active-Instrumental)
- Inquiry (Reflective-Instrumental)

four critical interpersonal issues—*trust,* a shared *focus* for dialogue or action, a *direction* or plan, and strategies for *action.*

However, business is more than an arena for bonding and attachment. It is comprised of situations, events, roles, and long-term processes that must be skillfully addressed. Gifted relating in a failing organization is a losing proposition. Therefore, interpersonal skills must support other business agendas too. To apply interpersonal skills, a leader must always address several themes simultaneously—the personal needs of individual relationships, the demands of day-to-day situations, and the demands of longer-term business cycles.

The 4-I model can show you what skill *mix* is most important to confront particular management situations. It can also show which skills are inappropriate distractions from the agenda at hand.

A third of all relating difficulties result from inappropriate or inadequate responses to situational demands. For example, one young manager related the following story illustrating a deficit of sensitivity:

> I was having a really bad week. Nothing had gone right for me. So when I came to work one day last week and Don greeted me by saying, "Good morning, how are you today?," I actually told him. I told him about my car breaking down, about my sore throat, about my project that's behind schedule. Finally, I noticed him fidgeting. He just wanted to be polite and expected me to say, "I'm fine . . . how are you?" He wasn't deeply wanting to know about everything in my life at that moment. I misunderstood what was going on.

Applying the 4-Is • 131

A map for leading embattled soldiers in a foxhole would have a unique landscape. It would require a lot of direction and very little questioning and indirect forms of influence. (See Figure 6–3.)

A map for the implementation phase of a project, in contrast, would demand directive influence to set goals, meet milestones, and confront problems and strategic influence to motivate and empower coworkers to complete tasks independently. Even though influence techniques are the focus in this case, notice that project leadership also requires ongoing interaction and inquiry. (Figure 6–4.)

The four quadrants can be conceptualizd as a "geography" of interpersonal skills. Each special context and business agenda requires covering part of the model's landscape. For example, developing a team identity with new members requires all four "regions" of the interpersonal skills map but mostly relies on interaction skills to

Figure 6–3: The 4-Is: Leading Embattled Soldiers

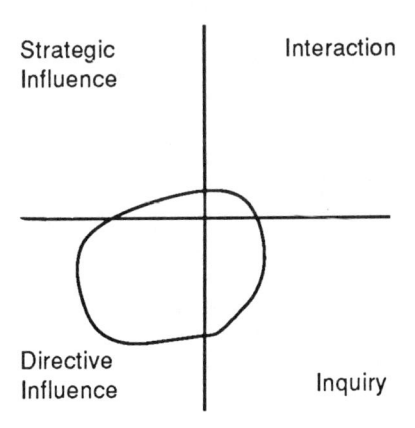

engender harmony and consensus. Therefore, a skills map for team formation might look like the picture in Figure 6–5.

The 4-Is: Team Formation

Many work situations depend heavily on the skillful movement or sequencing through the process required to confront the situation's issues. In these settings, a leader must be able to institute key steps and skillfully make transitions between steps. The focus on process—and movement—is particularly apparent in situations such as meetings, presentations, selling sessions, and negotiations.

Some situations, such as those where interaction skills are most important, depend more heavily on personal refinements of behavior that focus on the subtle details of a relationship. For example, coaching and counseling ses-

Figure 6–4: The 4-Is: Leading Project Implementation

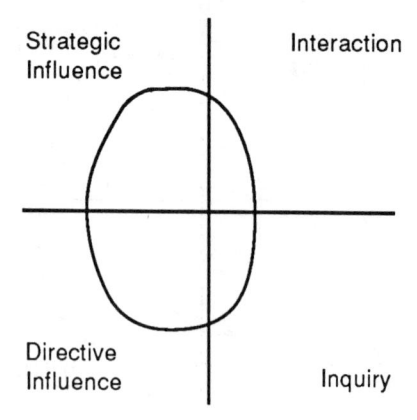

Strategic Influence | Interaction

Directive Influence | Inquiry

sions, which depend primarily on trust, should be supported by the finely tuned, attentive, abiding presence of the leader. A personal focus is required to demonstrate empathy, sensitivity, respect, and rapport.

As people mature, they play many roles and may work in several professions. Interpersonal skills must change accordingly. Excellence in each job is achieved when its own unique blend of interpersonal skills is successfully mastered. Therefore, although a particular job role contributes little to the choice of interpersonal skills moment to moment, it profoundly affects the kind of skill mix needed for long-term success.

The case of Nancy Vogel, a middle manager for a large financial services corporation, illustrates how a typical leader mixes and matches interpersonal skills during an average week.

Figure 6-5: The 4-Is: Team Formation

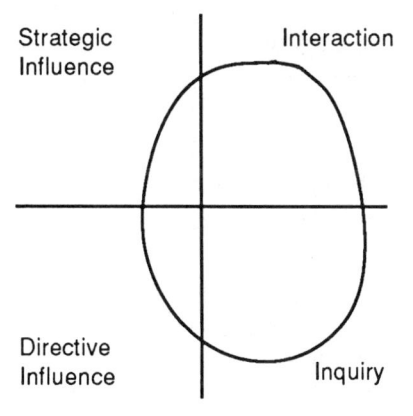

Strategic Influence | Interaction

Directive Influence | Inquiry

Monday: Keeping Mary Motivated

When Nancy came to work early on Monday, Mary was already getting organized. She was an energetic but somewhat insecure and nervous young woman who had saved Nancy's neck more than once. Before Nancy unloaded the usual list of problems, she greeted Mary. "How was your weekend?"

Mary responded hesitantly, "It was just OK. I went to the beach but got a pretty nasty sunburn. I was up half the night."

Nancy replied, "That's too bad. You know, you're kind of fair-skinned. Maybe you should use a sun screen."

Mary's mood cheered visibly, "I guess I should. I never learn. Every time I go to the beach I expect to be brown as a berry."

Nancy said, "Well, watch yourself. I really need your help here to keep things on track."

Mary smiled, "Thanks."

Nancy grimaced, as if laboring under the weight of her stack of papers. She plopped a pile of work on Mary's desk. "Here's what we're facing this week, and it's quite a bit: a presentation on the new equipment leasing project for senior staff on Wednesday, the project planning session with Don on Thursday, and a project team meeting for Friday."

Mary smiled again, "You're lucky you've got me."

"I know," Nancy agreed, nodding her head.

Nancy was lucky to have Mary as a resource. But the quality of her work depended on Nancy's attention. Mary's previous boss sometimes got annoyed at her small talk and her need for approval. In contrast, Nancy made sure to spend some time every day touching base—showing her respect, hearing about her concerns, making sure she knew she appreciated all the contributions she made. Nancy got her best effort because Mary felt Nancy really cared—she could rely on her to pay attention to their relationship.

Tuesday: Coaching Bill

Nancy's role as project leader required a lot of collaboration, mostly with people from other functions in her business, particularly marketing and sales. Bill, a financial analyst, was one of the few individuals reporting directly to her. Bill's role in the equipment leasing project was to supply Nancy with projections of the return on investments for various pieces of equipment, considering different constraints, such as changing interest rates and corporate tax laws. Bill was an adequate worker, but he had problems with a few key aspects of his job. Nancy decided to use Bill's annual performance review as an opportunity for coaching him.

Nancy invited Bill into her office, got him a cup of coffee, turned off the phone, and offered him a seat at a small circular table that would allow them to sit side by side rather than across an imposing desk. Nancy started. "Bill, this is your yearly performance review. There's been a lot of pressure with this new project, and I want to tell you how much I appreciate your being such a helpful team player."

Bill beamed; he always beamed when he got positive feedback. Nancy went on, "How do you think you've been doing your job?" Not only did Nancy show Bill respect by asking him, not telling him, about his work, but Nancy also encouraged a more collaborative dialogue. Long ago Nancy had learned that coworkers, particularly those like Bill, usually know most of their own assets and vulnerabilities. Given the opportunity, most people will confront their own work problems vigorously.

Bill outlined to Nancy some of his strengths and highlighted a few weaknesses, particularly his difficulty sorting through details to conceptualize things. Nancy pursued Bill's lead by asking a number of clarifying questions, such as, "How does the problem affect your work? What gets in the way of your changing? What steps might you take to confront this difficulty?" By using a series of open-ended questions, Nancy was able to specify some of Bill's difficulties without being too directive. Most important, Bill addressed Nancy's main concern—missing vital milestones and overlooking details after making firm commitments. By fostering an open, nonjudgmental exploratory discussion, Nancy also gave herself an opening for making some specific suggestions to Bill about managing deadlines.

Giving advice was not Nancy's forte; she hated being controlling or controlled. But by establishing a platform for open give-and-take and by using interaction skills to establish trust and inquiry skills to establish a focus to direction, Nancy was able to give pointed suggestions without being coercive or unkind. In this case, Nancy used directive influence only after establishing a firm relating foundation. She offered advice, asked Bill to focus on a few things to improve, and made sure she had Bill's understanding and commitment for self-improvement.

Wednesday: Presenting to Senior Staff

By Tuesday afternoon, Nancy was in a frenzy. As usual, her week was packed with minor crises, preventing her from completing preparations for the Wednesday presentation on the status of her project.

Nancy had become a master presenter. She was not a naturally charismatic orator but had learned how to prepare and how to view presentations as an interpersonal process.

Nancy had used a series of steps for developing her presentations, honed over a number of years. First, she decided what three or four points she wanted to highlight for her audience. One of the major flaws in most presentations stems from "firehosing" the audience with facts, figures, and general data overload. People can attend to only a few key concepts over a short time span. Next, Nancy usually wrote a script. This often required many drafts—one for flow, one for transition between key points, one for infusing variety in the material, one for staging, and one for impact. Most individuals omit one or more of these vital steps. Then, Nancy practiced—really practiced. She selected what to wear with great care. She determined what image she wanted to portray and then rehearsed every aspect of her talk aloud. She presented for timing and pacing. She organized the room, practiced using her visuals, and even noted points in the presentation for moving to different parts of the room and for audience participation. Too often, presenters forget that a talk is a special kind of two-way interchange. To produce the most impact, the speaker must engage his or her audience individually and collectively through a variety of techniques, such as eye contact, direct and rhetorical questions, body movement and position, and selective influence strategies embedded in the presentation script. Nancy always planned and mastered each of these steps before going on stage.

Thursday: The Project Update

Most developing leaders, like Nancy, have several project leadership roles over the span of their careers. This role is not only a prerequisite of successful businesses but also important for individual career development. It represents a bridge to an all-encompassing view of what makes businesses succeed. Leaders have to use interfunctional collaboration, goal completion through influence, and conceptual thinking to solve problems and make changes happen. In addition, they have to manage complex sets of tasks and solve multiple problems in a limited time frame.

The task skills required for project leadership are a specialized form of a management cycle. (See Figure 6–6.) Based on network planning, the group of task-oriented skills for project completion facilitate the planning, scheduling, and controlling of time-limited work problems. The group of network planning techniques, such as PERT, GANNT, GERT, and PDM, each track the multiple interrelationships among project parts. A network diagram is the result of planning but relies on a clear definition of objectives and specification of required activities to complete project tasks. Scheduling happens when you apply time estimates to each element of the network diagram. Project control comes from comparing actual progress with scheduled progress and then diagnosing and confronting the cause of discrepancies.

It's important to remember that all aspects of network planning and project tracking are merely methods of planning, diagnosing problems, and ensuring productive outcomes at each stage.

Nancy was a superior project leader. She was the kind of person who sees problems as challenges, even as opportunities. Most important, Nancy recognized that excellence in project leadership depends just as much on personal skills as it does on specific tools, techniques, and steps of project management. She recognized that every stage of a project relies on all interpersonal skills but that some stages require a more concentrated mix of particular skills.

Nancy was about half-way through setting up a com-

Figure 6-6: Project Management Cycle

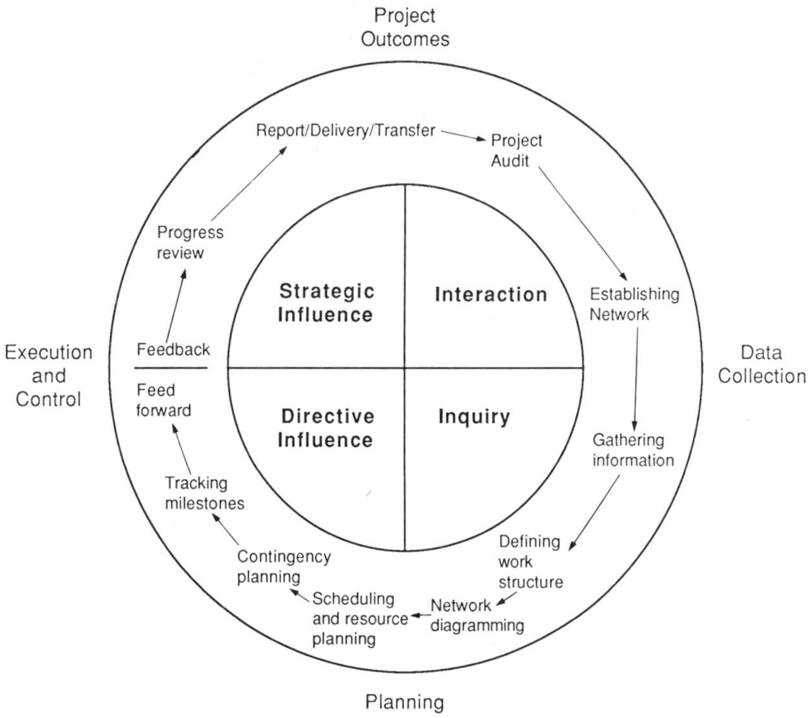

prehensive equipment leasing system. The project team had collected appropriate information, and it had developed a comprehensive plan with specific goals and milestones. Now the team was well into the implementation phase of the project. Although arguments and misunderstandings frequently spurred Nancy to use interaction and inquiry skills to reestablish trust and focus for action, she mostly needed to balance directive and strategic forms of influence to make sure she was using her co-workers as resources and getting the work finished on time and under budget.

Friday: Team Development

Nancy generally met with the equipment leasing project team every Friday morning. She had worked hard at developing team spirit. This was a particularly difficult task, since many of the team members were from different parts of the organization and because the composition of the team changed over time as new skills were needed.

A team can also be viewed as an open system that relies on many properties for successful functioning—leadership and membership skills, appropriate information flow and boundaries, and methods for ensuring productive work. Nancy saw team-building as one of her most critical tasks. Understanding that team growth was critical to the success of her project, she focused on assuring or reinforcing the critical functions and processes that make teams run. These can be simplified into four roles that members of an excellent team must demonstrate:

- *Harmonizing* or the process of developing an identity and consensus;

- *Exploring* or the process of discovering new ideas.
- *Regulating* or the process of developing defined boundaries through practices, policies, or procedures.
- *Producing* or the process of exporting work or information from inside the team.

Each of these roles is supported primarily by one of the four interpersonal skill groups. (See Figure 6–7.)

Figure 6-7: Four Team Roles

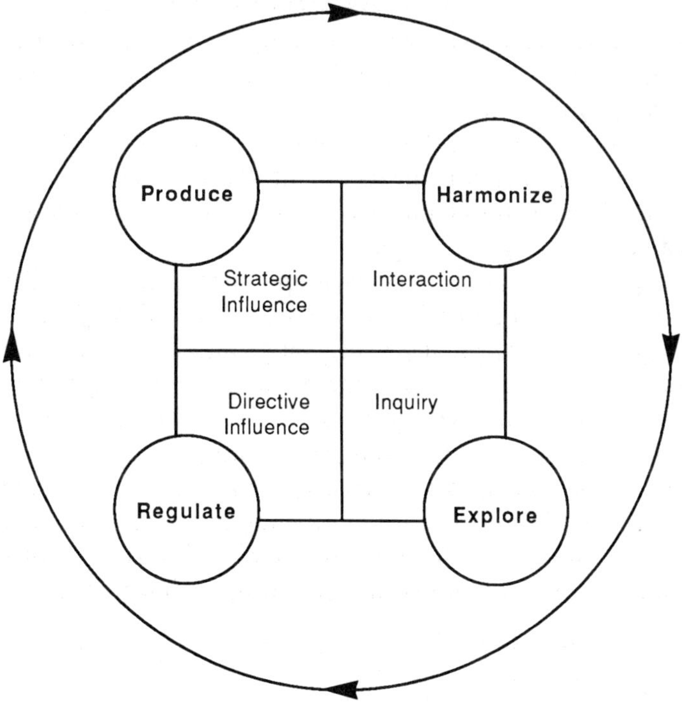

In developing roles, Nancy used interaction to help the group harmonize by fostering safety, appreciation, and open-mindedness. She used inquiry to help the group explore by asking questions, listening, and encouraging participation and dialogue.

She used directive influence to help them regulate by focusing on the tasks of the team and specific methods and plans for accomplishing them. Finally, she used strategic influence to help them produce by delegating responsibility and developing specialized roles. Nancy finished the week feeling satisfied. She knew she had five productive days in which she was able to practice her interpersonal skills and develop her coworkers too. But Nancy knew next week was a new opportunity for growth. It would surely bring new, largely unanticipated, interpersonal challenges.

Putting Interpersonal Skills to Work

Interpersonal skills have become the currency of effective relationships at work. They support all aspects of one-to-one interchanges, team efforts and organizational spirit. In order to maximize their impact, the most competent leaders consistently organize and plan their interpersonal activities through a series of steps. A wise senior manager stated, "As I've gotten older—and grown up some—I've learned how to succeed at relating. For one thing, I fail a lot. Bad moods, misunderstandings, real disagreement—they all cause trouble with other people. But a relationship isn't a moment or a single event; it's a pattern in which you keep trying and succeed a little more often than you don't."

What can you do in practical day-to-day terms to sponsor a creative, productive, and gratifying workplace? You can develop critical knowledge, skills, and attitudes about how people, organizations, and communications work. Effective leaders develop a spectrum of interpersonal strategies, each tailored to a practical here and now reality. To apply your interpersonal skills more effectively,

1. Acknowledge, understand, and tolerate the normal conflicts of the new workplace, suppress unrealistic expectations, and support the creative spirit of the individual worker;
2. Tailor skills to the person, the situation, and the group and organization setting (see Figure 6–8, p. 144);
3. Decide on an appropriate mix, sequences, and refinements of behaviors to fit specific interpersonal agendas;
4. Use individuals as mentors, friends, confidants, helpers, or group participants to sponsor individual growth and development in parallel with formally assigned tasks and roles;
5. Make people and relationships the most valued part of work.

These broad directives provide a way for each individual to develop and control his or her own world at work. The expression of psychological perspectives or individual organizational members is inevitable. Leaders can either view them as impediments to the logical, orderly, controlled business enterprise, or they can embrace the human aspects of the workplace as the primary resource for innovation and competitiveness. Because change is inevitable, as well as necessary, individuals who develop interpersonal skills as a primary resource will provide important leadership.

Figure 6-8: The 4-I Model of Interpersonal Skills: Applications

WHAT ↑

PEOPLE

Strategic Influence

Coworker's behavior
- Reticence
- Invested in status quo
- Not under direct control

Situation
- Project implementation
- Sales or marketing
- Negotiation
- Policy on strategy generation

Your role/job
- Project leader
- Transformational leader
- General manager/CEO

Interaction

Coworker's behavior
- Distrust
- New to the job or role
- Under stress

Situation
- Relationship-building
- Team-building
- Reaching consensus

Your role/job
- Coaching
- Counseling
- Personnel position

← **ACTIVE**   **REFLECTIVE** → **HOW**

Directive Influence

Coworker's behavior
- Poor quality work
- Passivity or reticence
- Overwhelmed

Situation
- Goal Setting
- Planning
- Milestones and deadlines
- Project implementation
- Crises
- Problem-solving

Your role/job
- Project leader
- Problem-solver
- Crisis manager
- Operations manager

Inquiry

Coworker's behavior
- Reticence/withdrawal
- Possessing vital information
- In trouble; having problems
- Having unmet needs

Situation
- Information-gathering
- Group or organizational diagnosis
- Problem definition
- Brainstorming or idea generation

Your role/job
- Problem-solver
- Entrepreneur
- Inventor
- Conceptualizer
- Consultant

THINGS ↓

7

Personalizing the 4-Is

Do It in Style: Developing a Personal Presence

Ideally, effective leaders adapt their own unique styles to each individual they manage. This acknowledges that each relationship is a complex, one-of-a-kind interaction in which both overt and covert communications occur all the time.

All leaders have a personality and an interpersonal style that pervades their day-to-day activities. Because these qualities are difficult if not impossible to change, what can leaders do to minimize the destructive effects of their own personality traits?

Fortunately, all people have a wide array of possible behaviors and significant volitional control over many of their actions. Therefore, anyone can improve his or her performance to a very great degree without a personality transformation.

The best leaders start by preparing for success. They are introspective about their own strengths and foibles and excellent at assessing their leverage in relationships with coworkers. In addition, the best performers take care of themselves. They develop their confidence and self-image. They pay attention to their physical well-being, style of speaking, and dress. For example, a presenter with a sensitive position in a marketing center undermined his interpersonal impact by wearing a toupee that didn't fit. One of his customers commented, "I tried to listen, but I couldn't keep my eyes off his head. I wondered where he got it, what it was made of, and if it would fall off or something. It looked precarious." In another case, a bright promising, young sales manager repeatedly hurt her credibility by using baby talk. She would use phrases such as "little bitty," "cutesie-wootsie," or "I gotta go wee wee." She was astonished when these negative behaviors were pointed out to her. These were isolated behaviors with a negative impact, but she was completely unaware of them.

The dimensions of self-care extend to surroundings too. The best leaders try to organize their lives, their time, their physical space, and the materials pertinent to their job (such as memos, reports, or agendas for meetings). Each of these "secondary channels" of communication can strongly support or detract from the effectiveness of interpersonal skills.

Along with removing the personal obstacles to interpersonal success, effective leaders prepare for relating. Some try to "visualize" themselves in specific situations before performing them. Some use more elaborate measures of rehearsal in which they practice aloud by themselves or role play situations with friends, family, or colleagues. No matter what methods you use, studies show that if you practice performance, you will increase personal confidence, comfort, and motivation and will improve your success in the situation.

Learning How to Grow

Tapping your already existing well of potential skills is an excellent start for improving your interpersonal effectiveness. But effective leaders also are not afraid to tackle change in areas where they are less competent. Just as organizations must change their values, practices, policies, and procedures to be competitive, their leaders must grow by acquiring new knowledge, skills, and attitudes. But how does a person know what to change? And once interpersonal vulnerabilities are discovered, what is the best way to ensure substantive, lasting change?

Effective learning is a process that includes several discrete steps, each playing an important role in consolidating new behavior. The basic learning cycle includes

- Motivating to learn;
- Defining a focus for change;
- Specifying the new behavior(s);
- Practicing the new behavior(s);
- Incorporating feedback;
- Refining the behavior(s);
- Personalizing the behavior(s).

At the core of any learning process is motivation—the intent to change. In all change processes, such as learning, counseling, and coaching, it has been discovered that the degree to which a person wants to change correlates more with success than almost any other factor. Therefore, if an individual wants to change or help others change, building motivation is the primary task. For interpersonal skills, this can be a surprisingly difficult pursuit because people's assumptions and concerns about relating can be deep-seated. For example, one young leader stated, "If you've got a mouth, you can relate." This young man may have suffered from arrogance or fear, but his attitude is widespread. Most individuals mistakenly assume that the skills they learned growing up are more than adequate. Other people assume that interpersonal skills are so nebulous that they cannot be understood or developed.

The 4-I model also helps individuals define a focus for mastering small but very helpful new interpersonal behaviors. The model helps individuals ask and answer the following questions for skill development:

- Do I have problems mixing, sequencing, or refining and personalizing behavior skills?
- Do I need to be more active, reflective, task-oriented, or people-oriented?
- What behaviors, strategies, or action steps should I improve?
- Am I having trouble establishing trust, diagnosing a focus for constructive activities, developing appropriate plans or directions, or generating effective ways of getting others to implement tasks?

The answer to these queries should provide important areas for self-improvement. In fact, most often people generate too many behaviors to change, each with too little definition. To change effectively, select only a few behaviors at a time. In addition, develop your proposed objectives by asking the following questions:

- How can I make the behaviors easy to learn? To make learning as easy as possible, some people limit the number of behaviors and write them down.
- How can I ensure that they're easy-to-use behaviors

and helpful on the job? People often test their proposed behavior change with a "partner in learning."
- How can I ensure that these behaviors have general application? Often, individuals can get a picture of how behaviors will work by reviewing how they will work in a variety of situations—for example, through rehearsal or role-playing.
- How can I make sure my investment of time and energy is worth it? Leaders must trust that they can change, that small changes will make a large difference, and that they can complete self-improvement projects with high impact.

The 4-I model is only a starting point for skill definition and development. Every person must translate the elements of the model into personal plans and initiatives. Moreover, all forms of skill development require practice. Effective practice requires not only a place where you can practice in privacy, a training environment, or a trusted partner in learning but also extensive experience in a natural working environment. Noel Tichy, from the University of Michigan, believes that 80 percent of a leader's development occurs on the job and 20 percent from formal study. One frustrated learner described his problems with trying new skills after a training session: "I understood what I needed to change, and I tried to do some new things a couple of times back on the job. But it was just too hard. I felt silly, and I couldn't tell what I was doing better and what wasn't going well. So after a few weeks I was back doing the same old things. That training I was so excited about turned out to be expensive entertainment and a week off from work. That's all."

In contrast, an individual who was a natural at self-improvement reported, "I've always been pretty successful. But not so great with people. I really work at that a lot. You ask what my secret is—I take care of all my failures; the successes take care of themselves." This second individual had learned that self-change requires many false starts, partial success, and outright failures. The difficulties are no greater than with other projects. They are much more personal. This often results in a real form of self-neglect. As one project manager in a manufacturing firm stated: "If I ran my projects the way I run myself, I'd fire me!"

To succeed at personal improvement requires persistence and commitment. Initial strategies and plans are always revised and refined from feedback, particularly the effects of the behavior on others. Furthermore, the most effective skills are the most personal. In other words, all interpersonal skills that are part of your change effort should be put into your own rules. For some people, this might take the form of an acronym to encompass a process or set of steps. For others, it might be a script with personal statements or quotes. The process of personalizing rules of behaviors makes the skills more memorable and adaptable.

Developing Interpersonal Resources

The best leaders model their commitment to interpersonal processes by demonstrating appropriate skills and self-improvement strategies. For example, a project leader of a factory automation effort noted: "I make sure I hold myself to the standard I apply to my team members. I always make sure to set a good example, to hold myself to the highest standards of behavior. Why? Because when I started out, I had a first boss who was full of baloney. He talked about a participatory workplace and then controlled everything. He talked about respect for coworkers and then repeatedly disregarded other people's suggestions. He knew all the buzz words but had no substance or soul."

Besides modeling the best practices, excellent leaders ensure a safe arena for development. They establish interpersonal skills as a value and sponsor risk-taking, honesty, and exploring relationships as a method for increasing quality of work life and productivity. The 4-I model supplies the principles and strategies for personal, team, and even organizational change. Leadership must supply the faith and energy required for ongoing development.

Putting It All Together

How should you put change principles into practice? One of the best methods is to use small self-improvement projects. This means defining a small problem to solve, specifying desired outcomes, setting appropriate goals, and writing an action plan with steps for practice, milestones, feedback procedures, methods for refinement and further practice, and an opportunity for review and skill consolidation.

For example, Dan, a manager of a human resources department in a large manufacturing firm, was put in charge of a leadership curriculum. This required multiple collaborations with people over whom he had no direct authority. Dan had a typical technical background and was used to managing his own technical tasks or directing a small team. He prided himself on being a "shop guy, direct and to the point." But now he was dealing with a wide range of people. He knew he had to improve his ability to influence. So Dan laid out the following plan:

- *Problem*: Improve strategic influence strategies.
- *Outcomes*: Ability to use a larger number of influence strategies with coworkers in a more skillful way, particularly
  1. To improve my ability to determine what will persuade others;
  2. To increase my ability to mount logical and emotional appeal during conversation.

After Dan determined his desired outcomes, he reviewed the 4-I model, particularly strategic influence, and determined that he needed to concentrate on three things: spending enough time asking open-ended questions during discussions in order to establish rapport and find out what matters to other people; using more persuasion and less direction; and completing all the steps required for effective influence. As a result, Dan set up the following goal:

- *Goal*: To practice my influence strategies in at least three discussions by next Friday.

Next, Dan outlined a plan for his first meeting. He chose Jim because Jim was an honest and forthcoming colleague and a friend.

- *Plan*:
  1. Arrange discussion with Jim about trainees' need for project leadership course;
  2. Outline the agenda early in the discussion;
  3. Focus on asking open-ended questions (i.e., what, why, how, etc.) to learn about Jim's perspective and problems.
  4. Avoid being too direct or directive; use at least three types of persuasion during the discussion.

5. Make sure to summarize any agreements.
6. Write an agenda employing the strategic influence key actions to use as a script during the meeting.
7. Ask Jim for feedback about how well I define his concerns and use influence techniques.

Dan arranged his meeting and faithfully followed his self-improvement steps. Or at least he thought he did. When asked to comment on their interchange, Jim was initially surprised. But he warmed to the task, reporting, "You know, Dan, you got what you wanted. But you're always in such a hurry. Those questions you asked me—it felt as if I was being grilled by the police."

Dan was a little shocked. "I thought I was using open-ended questions to get more information."

Jim replied, "Well, if you were, you should've moved a little slower. Give me a chance to think, to offer some answers I really mean."

Dan went on. "What about some of the persuasive techniques I was trying?"

"Good and bad," Jim responded. "I could really identify with your argument that loaning part of my staff would make our whole group look better. But you could have made a stronger case if you'd used a lot more persuasive techniques. It seems you always want to get to the bottom-line. For example, you could've traded favors. I could use your expertise in that design review next week. Or you could've appealed to some group values—or a higher authority, such as our boss's push to share resources."

After the meeting, Dan was full of mixed feelings. He didn't like failing very much, particularly when he had been so careful to plan for success. But he was elated too.

He was not only surprised at how forthcoming Jim had been but also at the clarity of his problems and their solutions. Subsequently, Dan rewrote his plan, incorporating suggestions discussed with Jim. In fact, with each attempt at practicing influence, Dan improved and developed specific, personal rules for correcting his vulnerabilities.

Dan's approach is unfortunately unusual. People most often relent to the pressure of work tasks and fail to allocate personal energy to self-improvement. However, you can develop your interpersonal skills while you work. This is the best way to learn.

Making Change a Habit

In the new workplace individual effort is the most valuable means of control, creativity, and growth. The person is now the locus of control and therefore the necessary focus of development efforts. Organizations now more closely approximate open systems—environments in which information and other resources are widely shared, crossing all the traditional inner and outer boundaries. No longer can leaders negotiate business life by rules and static policies. Small, face-to-face interventions and personal decisions make the difference. As a manager of marketing in a pharmaceutical firm noted, "I have a formal job title and I directly control some people. But we work in a 'matrix' environment. Most of the important work and important decisions occur between work functions or between people over whom I have no direct authority. So my effectiveness really depends on my personal skills—my ability to inspire trust, to influence, to form alliances and networks."

In today's work environment, flatter organizations often form new projects, programs, and structures to meet ever-changing worldwide market pressures. In this setting, personal competence in general and interpersonal skills in particular are prized resources.

Change is also a prerequisite for organizational survival and growing in the ability to relate skillfully is one of the critical types of change. This is the key to creating power and developing new ways of sharing and teaming. In short, both individuals and organizations must adopt a spirit of exploration and growth.

Improving Yourself: Analyzing the Context

Your own awareness of work surroundings can help sharpen your interpersonal effectiveness. To improve your ability to match interpersonal skills to context, choose a typical interchange with another individual at work:

1. First, *analyze the microenvironment.* Write out as many factors as you can using the following list of categories that influenced how you heard and were heard in the interaction. Specify how they helped or hindered communication. Pay special attention to
   - Colloquialisms
   - Verbal style
   - Dress
   - Body movements
   - Closeness/distance
   - Silence
   - Written documents
   - Facial expressions
2. Next, *focus on the personal environment.* Note as many factors as you can using the following list of

categories that influenced your relationship. Again, specify how they helped or hindered communication:
- Your personality style
- Your relating partner's style
- Your personal life issues
- Your partner's life issues
- Your self-image
- Your partner's self-image

3. Finally, *focus on the microenvironment.* List the factors influencing your relationship using the following categories. Specify how they affected relating:
   - Cultural values or rules
   - Team norms or values
   - Issues or problems in your work group
   - Physical work space

After reviewing the context factors that are affecting your relationship, use the summary tables at the end of each of the four core chapters to develop interpersonal strategies for confronting them.

Improving Yourself: Personal Change

It is important to remember that personal change is just as inevitable as organizational change. By taking a personal inventory, you can begin a commitment to growth. We offer you tools that can help fulfill this goal as you learn how to plan and execute personal and organizational change.

Every manager knows personal change is necessary in order to expand and develop leadership skills. This is neither easy nor simple. But we have observed successful individuals using the following guidelines to personalize strategies used in organizational change:

1. *Define.* Select one or more strategies or behaviors to change in order to improve your ability to confront a specific context, situation, or role demand. Write a one-sentence/statement to capture what skill or behavior you plan to change.
2. *Practice.* Choose an unthreatening setting that demands the skill or behavior, either in your job or at home (e.g., new team assignments, a house renovation, marital discussion). Write down a few simple, practical action steps. Make sure they fit both your setting and your personality.
3. *Review.* Then take a few minutes to review your strategies with a coworker or family member. Make sure to take the time to explain exactly what you are trying to do and ask for feedback about how well they think your interventions will work. For example, you might ask
   - How can I adapt the strategies to be more effective?
   - What are the potential pitfalls?
   - How can I translate strategies into specific behavioral steps?
   - What problems might I neglect or bypass?
4. *Test and practice.* Test and refine your personal interventions by asking the following questions and then trying them in a relatively nonthreatening setting:
   - Are your strategies simple?
   - Can they be practiced frequently on the job?
   - Can they be expressed by you in a clear, meaningful way?
   - Can you evaluate how you are doing with personal goals for improvement through feedback discussions with others and/or through intermittent com-

parisons of your performance on the job (e.g., at monthly intervals)?
5. *Personalize.* After practicing the skills, rewrite your plans and generate a short list of "personal rules" for self-improvement.

Remember, knowledge alone is not enough for change. But by constant practice, you can become a model of personal change and maximize your effect on your peers, your team, and your organization.

Epilogue: Fit to Lead

A New Age: A New Challenge
"Economic performance is the specific function and contribution of business enterprise, and the reason for its existence."
—Peter Drucker from *Managing for Results,* Pan Books, London, 1967, p. 9.

"The whole individual raises new problems for the organization, partly because of the needs of his own personality, partly because he brings with him a set of established habits . . . and commitments to special groups outside the organization."
—P. Selznick, 'Foundations of the Theory of Organizations, *American Sociological Review,*Vol. 13, 1948, pp. 25–35.

We are experiencing a period of great change. The revolution in information flow and other technologies, along with a truly global economy, have transformed the workplace into an environment open to new ways of doing business. Organizational structures and policies have lost much of their power to control economic agendas. The paternalistic organization is now a thing of the past—neither life-long employment nor protection are forthcoming.

Organizations embody conflicting perspectives and purposes and this particularly true in this era of technological and cultural change. Inconsistency and uncertainty are constant companions. Experts even use terms such as turbulence and "messes" to describe today's workplace. These realities are seldom acknowledged, much less confronted. Business systems, driven by organizational goals, often take on a life of their own. From their perspective, people are sometimes considered a necessary, but flawed instrument of this purpose. Their feelings and eccentricities are not only unpredictable and highly resistant to change, but also are frequently in conflict with overt and covert organizational goals. To business, the powerful needs of people, their subjective perceptions, and emotional investments impede organizational efficiency and need to be managed, suppressed, expunged.

Most of the time, organizations conduct an ambivalent and only partially successful effort to promote the productivity and growth of its participants. On the one hand, they pay lip service to the human condition by halfheartedly sponsoring the development of individual workers and sympathetic leadership. On the other hand, policies, procedures, and processes are developed that control all elements of the business endeavor. At a practical level, this conflict is resolved by focusing on tasks—observable, reproducible, manageable, controllable, and predictable. Function, action, and bottom-line results are rewarded, revered, and theoretically enshrined. But, there is a flaw which can turn short-term gains into inexorable, long-term failures. Rensis Likert and others have shown that neglected human resources significantly decrease business profitability over a period of years.

The focus on tasks to the exclusion of the whole person is a compelling reality. Standard management wisdom states that leaders should attend "to objective job standards, not subjective opinions". . . . "to variances, not personalities," "to behaviors, not feelings,". . . . "to documented organizational goals, and not people." When psychological approaches are incorporated into organizational culture—and this is an infrequent occurrence—they have done so at such a simple and rudimentary level, that they most often produce distortions and not solutions to the human problems encountered.

This is mostly an outgrowth of the illusion that leaders can and must control as many aspects of organizational life as possible. But, most often, these allegedly clear-headed principles miss two fundamental truths about business environments:

(1) That there are conflicts, often unresolvable in nature, between individual, group, and organizational goals.
(2) That any business reality is only a perception, constructed by human beings out of their ideas, emotions, beliefs, and context.

The complexities of conflicts in an organization are sometimes decried, and sometimes ignored, but seldom are seen as an ever-shifting reality to be accepted and confronted.

Unfortunately, human nature also conspires to cloud our understanding of the relationship between employees and organizations. Leaders and managers are people, subject to the same fears and vulnerabilities as their subordinates, prompting them to focus on tasks that can be mastered rather than complex, human interactions that cannot. Every manager worries, quite appropriately, that entering the world of genuine, honest, emotional relationships will lead to significant distractions from work and an inevitable web of emotional entanglements. Managers contend that the cost is too great. Most often, this is a response to anxiety about losing control of oneself, of one's position, of one's secure assumptions.

But what is the cost of not confronting people's hopes, fears, personalities, and the distortions they encounter in day-to-day human interactions? What is the cost of allowing business systems and its functions to dominate all business activity?

In the final analysis, every organization must cope with one critical concept—that it is a social system in which people problems, people skills and people resources ultimately determine its viability. In early industrial settings, the human scale of the workplace could be suppressed or avoided for very long periods of time. A production-line mentality (or reality) with its emphasis on interchangeable parts and interchangeable people frequently worked for extended periods of time. Today, many businesses still naively assume that "human resources" are interchangeable with all other functions and behaviors of an organization's parts. Unfortunately, this is a fundamental misunderstanding. When you move from the world of things to the world of human perceptions, potentials, and actions, you have entered a new reality—one with new rules and new potentials. In fact, people's perceptions, even in the ways that they conflict with organizational practices, are the primary source of creative energy.

As the open exchange of information and communication become the currency of business, human interactions and their ability to change systems are at a premium. In this setting, both the synergism and the conflicts between person and organization are more evident and more pertinent. Manipulation, personal interests, subjective viewpoints, and psychological distortions cannot be avoided, even for one second.

A New Commitment

Paradoxically, the forces at work offer more *opportunity* and more *responsibility* for each individual. Personal competence and personal development are now more than ever the responsibility of every single person. Personal effectiveness is now a more vital and highly valued quality than ever before. In this setting, interpersonal skills will become the factor that discriminates among leaders. For those with the vision to select and nurture interpersonal skills as any other resource, tomorrow will provide new and exciting opportunities for creativity and teamwork.

Leaders cannot control these realities, but they can be knowledgeable, honest, influential participants in a communication process that facilitates growth and wisdom. By envisioning a business as an "adaptive coping system" that can meet both individual and organizational needs, leaders with the best interpersonal skills can contain conflicts and ensure openness to new ideas while maintaining boundaries for protection, develop productive goals and plans and influence coworkers to produce excellent work output.

This book provides a personal approach for meeting

the challenges of our new age. Based on studies of the competencies required of today's and tomorrow's leaders, it offers a method, a potential—nothing more. You must decide how to use the 4-I model and its lessons. You must decide to make the commitment to change and grow.

APPENDIX

The 4-I Interpersonal Skills Model and Inventory

Interpersonal skills support all leadership and strategic business interventions. They represent one of the vital keys for developing a more productive workplace. However, to develop interpersonal skills, we must have accurate, easy-to-use methods for assessment, understanding, coaching, training, and self-development. To do this, we have formulated and tested a simple interpersonal skills model—called the 4-I Model of Interpersonal Skills. Focusing on an individual's interpersonal skills related to specific job contexts, the companion self-relating inventory—the 4-I Interpersonal Skills Inventory—was used to generate and refine the model.

Preliminary Model Formation

In order to develop a simple framework for assessing and applying interpersonal skills, we started by completing an extensive review of the interpersonal skills literature. We primarily used counseling, psychotherapy, and business references and competency studies as sources. Any behaviors considered important for forming, maintaining, or influencing relationships were recorded and then translated into behavioral statements. Thereafter, they were grouped according to their similarities. Overlapping statements were eliminated or incorporated into other statements.

The final group of statements included over 100 behaviors, which could be defined by a few key characteristics. Each state-

166 • MANAGING TO RELATE

ment had a context or focus dimension, such as an orientation toward feelings or facts or concepts. Each statement also had a process dimension related to the stance taken by the person, from very active to very reflective. By assuming that these factors represented two dimensions—focus and process—a graph with four quadrants can be generated to portray all interpersonal skills (see Figure A–1).

After reviewing the nature of the four quadrants and statements pertinent to each one, they were labeled—interaction, inquiry, directive influence, and strategic influence. This graph and the four skill clusters formed the initial 4-I model.

Figure A–1: The 4-I Model of Interpersonal Skills

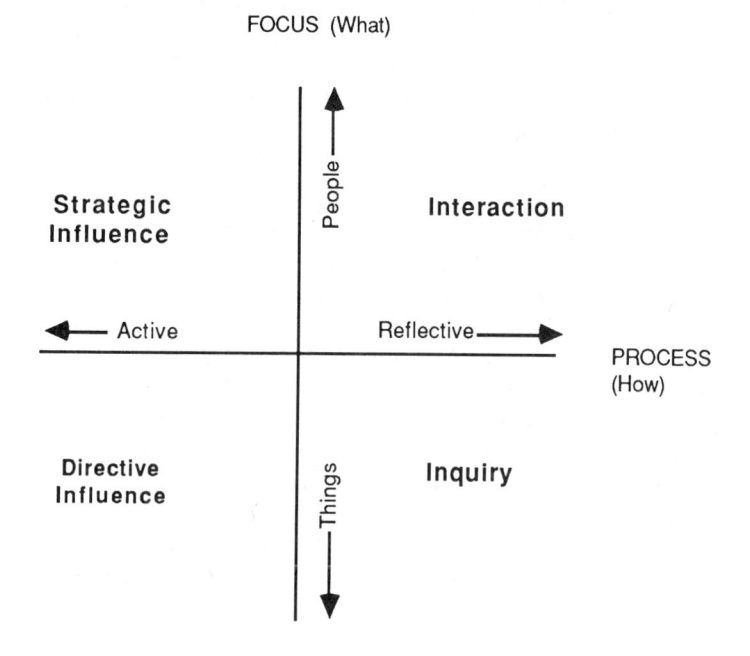

```
                    FOCUS (What)
                         ↑
                         │
                       People
    Strategic            │         Interaction
    Influence            │
                         │
    ←── Active ──────────┼───────── Reflective ──→   PROCESS
                         │                            (How)
    Directive            │         Inquiry
    Influence          Things
                         │
                         ↓
```

Model and Inventory Refinement

After developing a preliminary distribution of more than 100 behavioral statements among the four quadrants, we used a panel of six experienced behavioral scientists, who were unaware of our hypothesized model, to rate the behavioral statements according to the two dimensions. This initial test resulted in a general agreement about the location of various skill behaviors in the model but defined many items that were subject to misinterpretation or differences of opinion regarding their location along the two dimensions. These items were discarded or refined.

Thereafter, we began formal data collection. It proceeded in three stages. During the first, we asked participants in a project management course to rate seventy-six behavioral items—using the following instructions:

> Rate the following statements 1, 2, 3, or 4 according to how well each characterizes you in your present job role.
>
> 1 = Not very characteristic
> 2 = Somewhat characteristic
> 3 = Generally characteristic
> 4 = Very characteristic

Initial data analysis showed a promising tendency for some items to distribute along a dimension—generally corresponding to the active versus reflective dimension. The hypothesized dimension based on the content of interpersonal interventions was not well differentiated by the first administration of the inventory. Before a second group of administrations, we rewrote several items to further clarify their meaning based on data analysis. A similar procedure was followed to clean inventory items before a third set of administrations.

Model and Inventory Testing

The version of the interpersonal skills inventory reported in this appendix contained the forty-seven behavioral statements listed below.

Behavioral Statements
1. I give bad news in a direct, honest way.
2. I skillfully compromise differences of opinion.
3. I tailor the way I present ideas to fit other people's needs.
4. I dramatize situations to produce a positive impact.
5. I provide frequent, direct advice to keep things on track.
6. I persistently focus people on results.
7. I confront problems head on.
8. I reframe ideas into new perspectives.
9. I warn others about repercussions from their actions.
10. I suspend judgment during conversation.
11. I remain attentive and receptive during interactions.
12. I invest my full attention to interactions with others.
13. I use my optimism and energy to move things along.
14. I tell people exactly what I want them to do and why.
15. I am respectful of other people's ideas and opinions.
16. I reflect other people's thoughts and feelings back to them.
17. I purposely use silence and pauses to encourage conversation.
18. I time what I say and do in order to increase my impact on other people.
19. I order or organize priorities for others.
20. I get others to do things by promising a future payoff.
21. I express ongoing interest and warmth toward others.
22. I tune into the hidden meanings and feelings that underlie what people say.
23. I set up expectations for a future payoff.
24. I take charge to get things moving or overcome obstacles.
25. I am very open about my motives, intentions, problems.
26. I focus interactions on specific topics.
27. I selectively reward behaviors in others that correspond most to the things I want them to do.
28. I refer to esteemed values or common principles or respected opinions to convince.
29. I assert my opinions openly.
30. I summarize conversation and key interactions with others.

The 4-I Interpersonal Skills Model and Inventory

31. I repeat and restate statements of other people to encourage exploration.
32. I solicit a wide range of inputs from others.
33. I interpret the meaning of interactions and concerns.
34. I focus on other people's feelings and perceptions.
35. I give detailed directions for getting things done.
36. I paraphrase other people's statements.
37. I use close-ended and factual questions to specify and clarify.
38. I keep dialogue flowing with nonverbal encouragement (e.g., nod of head).
39. I demonstrate or illustrate desired behaviors.
40. I disclose feelings or special information to win the support of others.
41. I admit my concerns or confusions.
42. I let people know exactly what I expect of them.
43. I am calm, relaxed, and attentive during conversation.
44. I simplify concepts by focusing on their primary meanings.
45. I respond to and validate other people's opinions and feelings.
46. I use logical, emotional, or inspirational arguments to get my way.
47. I find ways to pass authority or responsibility to others that inspire high quality of work.

The inventory was administered to several hundred individuals at various companies. The data presented here are from a sample of sixty-nine individuals in two different training sessions. Most respondents were engineers; others were managers, supervisors, and scientists.

Interpersonal Skills Dimensions: Factor Analysis

A principal components factor analysis yielded strong support for the 4-I model of interpersonal skills. The analysis, constrained to identify four factors, was able to explain 40 percent of the common variance of the items with these four factors;

the eigenvalues of these factors ranged from 2.5 to 8.4; and item loadings or the factors corresponded largely to those predicted *a priori*. Most important, very significant loading (i.e., greater than .5) was demonstrated by most of the behavioral items for all four factors. The percentage of variance explained by each factor ranged from a high of 18, for the factor containing the directive influence items, to a low of 5 for the inquiry factor. (See Table A–1).

Interaction skills were assessed with responses to ten statements. Only one of these statements did not receive a loading of at least .3 on the interaction factor. Five statements assumed to measure other skill clusters received loadings of at least .3 on the interaction factor; just two of these (items 8 and 2) received their highest loading on interaction rather than the hypothesized skill cluster. (See Table A–2.)

Twelve statements were used to measure inquiry skills. Of these, ten received a loading of at least .3 on the inquiry factor. Of the statements with loadings of at least .3 on the inquiry factor, (items 30, 8, and 9), three statements were attributed *a priori* to other dimensions because of higher loadings on other factors. Seven remaining statements characterized Inquiry. (See Table A–3.)

Table A–1: Factor Analysis Statistics

FACTOR	EIGENVALUE	PERCENTAGE OF VARIANCE	CUMULATIVE PERCENTAGE
Directive influence	8.35390	17.8	17.8
Interaction	5.29037	11.3	29.0
Strategic influence	2.88975	6.1	35.2
Inquiry	2.47592	5.3	40.4

Table A-2: Factor Loadings for Interaction Statements

	INTERACTION	INQUIRY	DIRECTIVE INFLUENCE	STRATEGIC INFLUENCE
15. I am respectful of others' ideas and opinions.	.67697			
10. I suspend judgment during conversation.	.66633			
11. I remain attentive and receptive during interactions.	.62528			
45. I respond to and validate others' opinions and feelings.	.60398			
34. I focus on others' feelings and perceptions.	.60276			.37942
21. I express ongoing interest and warmth toward others.	.60202			.44888
43. I am calm, relaxed, and attentive during conversation.	.53871			
12. I invest my full attention to interactions with others.	.52615			
22. I tune into the hidden meanings and feelings that underlie what people say.	.47270			
8. I reframe ideas into new perspectives.[a]	.46773	.43942		
2. I skillfully compromise differences of opinion.[b]	.45263	.44165		
17. I purposely use silence and pauses to encourage conversation.[a]				.38411

[a] Items initially hypothesized as belonging to the inquiry cluster.
[b] Item initially hypothesized as belonging to the directive influence cluster.

Table A–3: Factor Loadings for Inquiry Statements

	INTERACTION	INQUIRY	DIRECTIVE INFLUENCE	STRATEGIC INFLUENCE
31. I repeat and restate statements of others to encourage exploration.		.68142		
36. I paraphrase others' statements.		.61305		
32. I solicit a wide range of inputs from others.		.61050		
37. I use close-ended and factual questions to specify and clarify.	.32125	.56001	.31225	
41. I admit my concerns or confusions.		.53526		
44. I simplify concepts by focusing on their primary meanings.		.47174	.31003	
16. I reflect others' thoughts and feelings back to them.	.33800	.39663		

Fourteen statements were included in the inventory to measure directive influence skills. All but one of these statements (item 2) received a loading of at least .3 on the directive influence factor; only two of these statements also received a loading of at least .3 on another factor (items 1 and 9). A total of seven statements that were presumed to measure other dimensions received loadings of at least .3 on directive influence, but three of these received higher loadings on other factors. (See Table A–4.)

Of the eleven statements used to measure strategic influence skills, nine received loadings of at least .3 on the corresponding factor and only two of these also received high loadings on another factor (items 18 and 46). Six items attributed to other dimensions received loadings of at least .3 on the strategic influence factor, although all but two of these (items 38 and 33) received higher loadings on other factors. (See Table A–5.)

The only statement out of the entire forty-seven that had a loading of .5 or higher on a factor other than the one for which it was noted in the hypothesized 4-I model was: "I keep dialogue flowing with nonverbal encouragement (e.g., nod of the head)." Although intended as a measure of inquiry skills, its loading of .65 on the strategic influence factor probably reflects its more active, assertive character than the other statements that made up the inquiry dimension.

Interpersonal Skill Dimensions: Reliability Analysis

Reliability analysis of the scales constructed from the sets of statements initially attributed to the four dimensions yielded satisfactory alpha coefficients in each case. Alpha values ranged from a high of .85 for directive influence to a low of .74 for inquiry and strategic influence. (See Table A–6.)

Scale Characteristics

The central tendency and variability of the four scales were similar and their shape was roughly normal. In other words,

Table A–4: Factor Loadings for Directive Influence Statements

	INTERACTION	INQUIRY	DIRECTIVE INFLUENCE	STRATEGIC INFLUENCE
42. I let people know exactly what I expect of them.			.77359	
19. I order or organize priorities for others.			.75101	
24. I take charge to get things moving or overcome obstacles.			.74265	
35. I give detailed directions for getting things done.			.71848	
14. I tell people exactly what I want them to do and why.			.71136	
29. I assert my opinions openly.			.66546	
5. I provide frequent, direct advice to keep things on track.			.62009	
5. I persistently focus people on results.			.53224	

39. I demonstrate or illustrate desired behaviors.		.51346	
7. I confront problems head on.		.51319	
47. I find ways to pass authority or responsibility to others that inspire high quality of work.[a]		.42459	.38797
9. I warn others about repercussions from their actions.	.32735	.41583	
30. I summarize conversation and key interactions with others.[b]	.33559	.40510	.35482
26. I focus interactions on specific topics.[a]		.39937	
13. I use my optimism and energy to move things along.		.34294	
1. I give bad news in a direct honest way.[a]	.32500	.32547	
25. I am very open about my motives, intentions, problems.[b]		.31350	

[a] Items initially hypothesized as belonging to the strategic influence cluster.
[b] Items initially hypothesized as belonging to the inquiry cluster.

Table A-5: Factor Loadings for Strategic Influence Statements

	INTERACTION	INQUIRY	DIRECTIVE INFLUENCE	STRATEGIC INFLUENCE
38. I keep dialogue flowing with nonverbal encouragement (e.g., nod of head).[a]				.64854
28. I refer to esteemed values, common principles, or respected opinions to convince.				.66633
40. I disclose feelings or special information to win the support of others.				.61050
23. I set up expectations for a future payoff.				.52957
20. I get others to do things by promising a future payoff.				.50843
27. I selectively reward behaviors in others that correspond most to the things I want them to do.				.49047
18. I time what I say and do in order to increase my impact on others.	.33594			.46304
33. I interpret the meaning of interactions and concerns.[b]				.44036
46. I use logical, emotional, or inspirational arguments to get my way.			.40351	.41372
3. I tailor the way I present ideas to fit others' needs.				.35614
4. I dramatize situations to produce a positive impact.				

[a] Items initially hypothesized as belonging to the inquiry cluster.
[b] Item initially hypothesized as belonging to the interaction cluster.

Table A-6: Reliability Analysis

SCALE	ALPHA
Directive influence	.85
Interaction	.80
Strategic influence	.74
Inquiry	.74

N = 66

they tended to show an appropriate "normal distribution" in the rating process. Item rating means ranged from 2.8 for interaction to 2.4 for strategic influence. The standard deviation for interaction was .52; standard deviations for the other scales were between .43 and .47. The inquiry scale had a slight negative skew; the directive influence scale, a slight positive skew; the other two had more normal distributions. (See Table A–7.)

Interscale Correlations

The highest interscale correlation, .56, was between inquiry and interaction; the lowest, .16, between interaction and directive influence. The other three interscale correlations ranged from .35 to .48 with the strategic influence scale showing

Table A-7: Scale Statistics

SCALE	MEAN	S.D.	SKEW	N
Interaction	2.8	.52	.08	68
Inquiry	2.7	.43	.38	69
Directive influence	2.7	.47	.22	67
Strategic influence	2.4	.45	.06	69

moderate correlation with each of the other scales. In other words, interaction and inquiry behaviors are demonstrated together more often than other combinations of skill clusters. Interaction and directive influence appear to be the most disparate types of interpersonal skills. And strategic influence, as hypothesized in the concept called "reintegration" (i.e., building and rebuilding skills in a predictable hierarchy), seems to employ behaviors from other skill clusters to support its own unique set of behaviors.

4-I Model and Inventory: Implications and Future Directions

The results from multiple studies and data analysis give compelling support for the 4-I Model of Interpersonal Skills. In addition, the studies support various theoretical aspects of the model:

- There are four very distinct interpersonal skills clusters—interaction, inquiry, directive influence, and strategic influence.
- The similarities can be found along the focus and process dimensions between skill clusters located adjacent to one another in the model;
- The dissimilarities lie between skill clusters not adjacent on the two dimensions (i.e., interaction versus directive influence); and
- The "integrative" nature of strategic influence causes it to use all skills to a significant degree to produce impact on others.

The studies also showed that a simple model can describe complex interpersonal behaviors and that simple, self-rated behavioral statements can be used to rate interpersonal skills anchored in a specific job context.

Perhaps most exciting, the 4-I interpersonal skills inventory suggests many possibilities for future study, including:

- Determining appropriate skill mixes for different situations, job contexts, or careers;
- Discriminating between excellent and average or poor performers in interpersonal skills in various job-related contexts; and
- Developing a simpler inventory with fewer items that better discriminate interpersonal skills.

The inventory, particularly since it has proven effective in a self-rating form, should be a helpful and easy-to-use tool for assessing and developing the kind of personal leadership required for future competitiveness.

Index

Achievement, 114
  oriented, 9
Action, 18, 71, 112
Advice, 78, 85, 86
Affiliation, 35, 113
  oriented, 9
Analysis, factor, 169
Application of interpersonal skills, 144
Applying the 4-I's, 127
Assertiveness, 79
Attachment, 27, 106, 107, 130
Attention, 25, 28–30, 46, 134, 135
Attentiveness, 29

Behaviors, 16–17
  empathic, 33
  responsive, 32
Body language, 26, 29, 30, 31, 55, 56

Career development, 6
Change, 1, 4, 144, 148, 160, 164
  habit, 156
  personal, 154–58
Charisma, 103, 115
Clarification, 51, 68–71, 72

Closed questions, 51, 61
Coaching, 6, 23, 43, 116, 132, 135–36
Commitment, 70, 91–92, 163, 164
Communication, channels, 16, 30
  covert, 29
  nature of, 11–12
  vehicle, 12
Competence, 163
Compromise, 38
Conceptualization, 51, 64–67, 72
Confrontation, 78, 90–91
Consensus, 140
Context, 127, 155–56
  analyzing, 155
Contingency management, 117, 119
Control, 105, 126, 161, 162
Controlling statements, 86–87
Counseling, 6, 23, 132
Creativity, 64, 114, 162, 163
Cue sensitivity, 29

Delegation, 103, 121
Dialogue, structured, 84
Direction(s), 18, 80
  charting, 81
  future, 178–79

Directive influence, 15, 76, 79, 80, 174–75
  application and limitations, 97
  key actions, 98
  payoff: structuring activities, 96
  strategies, 99–100
Disclosure, 109

Empathy, 26, 32, 36, 46
Empowerment, 103, 121–22, 125
Encouragement, 58–60
Environment, 107
Ethics, 12, 39
Eye contact, 30

Factor analysis, 169
  statistics, 170
Feedback, 23, 103, 117–21, 125
  negative, 117, 119, 179
  process, 20

Goals, 78, 83, 84, 85, 94, 95, 96, 97, 163
Goal setting, 84–85
"Group think", 27

Helping roles, 55

Influence, directive. *See* Directive influence
  gathering, 48, 54
  masters, 101
  strategic. *See* Strategic influence
Innovation, 9, 15, 64, 144
Interaction, 9, 15, 23, 171
  applications and limitations, 44
  correlations, 177
  key actions, 45
  strategies, 46
Interpersonal resources, 150
  skills model, 128
Inquiry, 15, 48, 172
  applications and limitations, 72
  key actions, 73
  payoff, 71
  strategies, 75
Inventory, refinement, 167
  testing, 167

Job satisfaction, 2

Leader(s)
  effective, 95
  organizing, 83
Leadership, 4, 6, 159, 163
  interventions, 128
  project, 5, 134–41
Learning, 147–52
  cycle, 147
Likert, Rensis, 160
Listening, 9, 48, 52–61, 72
  barriers, 54
  overlistening, 60
  vulnerabilities, 53

Management, contingency, 119
  cycle, 19, 20, 128, 129
  participative, 2
Manipulation, 104, 119
  of context, 117
Mentorship, 19
Mirroring, 31, 33
Model, 4–Is, application, 143
  4–Is of interpersonal skills, 166
Modeling, 109, 151
Morale, 2
Motivation, 22, 107, 112–15, 147

Motives, 107, 108, 112, 113, 114, 115

Negotiation, 132
Non-verbal cues, 30, 87, 88. See body language

Open questions, 62
Organization(s), 78, 81, 82, 85, 160
Organizing leaders, 83
Ownership building, 5

Participative management, 2
Paternalism, 3
"People power," 121
Performance review, 135–36
Personalizing the 4-Is, 145
Persuasion, 5, 103, 112–16, 125
Planning, 134–41
Plans, 21, 85, 86, 90, 95, 105, 163
Power motive, 103, 115
Power, sharing, 122
Presentations, 116, 132, 136–37
Priorities, 21
Project, implementation, 132
  leadership, 5, 136
  management, 134–41
  management cycle, 139
Punishment, 117, 118–19

Quality circles, 2
Questioning, 51, 61, 72
Questions, close-ended, 51, 61
  open-ended, 62, 86, 136

Rapport, 9, 26, 39–42, 41, 46
Reciprocal, 27, 40
Reflection, 23
Reinforcement, positive, 117
  intermittent, 120
Reintegration, 126
Relating, 13, 17
Relationship(s), 20
  building, 23
  collaborative, 20
  complementary, 27
Reliability analysis, 177
Respect, 26, 37–39, 46
Responsive behaviors, 32
Rewards, 117
Role, helping, 55

Scale characteristics, 173–74
Self-image, 146
Selling, 132
Selznick, P., 159
Shaping, 117–18
Sharing, 103, 108–12, 125
  feelings, 110
Skill development, 148–50
Skills
  directive influence, 78, 80
  inquiry, 52
  interaction, 27–28, 113
  mix, refine, sequence, 20, 116–20
  strategic influence, 103, 108
Strategic influence, 15, 101, 106, 176
  applications and limitations, 123
  key actions, 124
  payoff, implementing through people, 122
  strategies, 125
  and work motives, 107
Strategic thinking, 4
Structured dialogue, 84
Symmetrical relationships, 27
Systems, 2, 94, 140, 160, 162

Team-building, 5, 43, 131–32
Team, development, 140–42
  formation, 23, 132–33
  roles, 140–41
  spirit, 35, 37, 80, 107
Teamwork, 163
Tolerance, 20
Tracking, 78, 93–94

Trust, 18, 23, 26, 28, 33, 37
  building, 42–43, 51

Validation, 13
Verbal, communication, 9
  encouragement, 58–60
Vision, 4–5
Vulnerability
  genuineness, 33
  openness, 109

If you have questions about the 4I Model or interpersonal skills training you can contact Dr. Stephen C. Schoonover at 20 Randolph Road, Chestnut Hill, MA 02167 or at (617) 731-8458.

Addison-Wesley Training Systems will publish the 4–I Interpersonal Skills Inventory in Summer, 1988. For more information on this product or to order write:

Addison-Wesley Training Systems
Route 128
Reading, Massachusetts 01867

or call (617) 944–3700, extension 2714.

HF
5548.8　Schoonover, Stephen
.S353　　C.
1988
　　　　Managing to rela-
　　　　te

DUE DATE